WORDS OF COMFORT
FOR EVERY DAY

"I Love You, Lord"

"God is love, and whoever abides in love abides in God, and God in him" (1 Jn 4:16).

WORDS OF COMFORT
FOR EVERY DAY

"I Love You, Lord"

MINUTE MEDITATIONS FEATURING
SELECTED SCRIPTURE TEXTS
AND SHORT PRAYERS TO THE LORD

By Rev. Joseph T. Sullivan

Illustrated

CATHOLIC BOOK PUBLISHING CORP.
New York

CONTENTS

NIHIL OBSTAT: Francis J. McAree, S.T.D.
Censor Librorum

IMPRIMATUR: ✠ Patrick J. Sheridan, D.D.
Vicar General, Archdiocese of New York

The Nihil Obstat and Imprimatur are official declarations that a book or a pamphlet is free of doctrinal or moral error. No implication is contained therein that those who have granted the Nihil Obstat and Imprimatur agree with the contents, opinions or statements expressed.

(T-186)

ISBN 978-1-937913-05-2

INTRODUCTION

"In this is love, not that we have loved God but that He has first loved us and sent His Son to be the atoning sacrifice for our sins" (1 Jn 4:10).

The goal of living is to love God perfectly. This is everyone's calling. Jesus summed up all the commandments by saying:

"You shall love the Lord your God with your whole heart, and with your whole soul, and with your whole mind. This is the first and greatest commandment. And the second is like it; you shall love your neighbor as yourself" (Mt 22:36).

Christ also declared, "If you love Me, you will keep My commandments" (Jn 14:15).

St. Theresa of The Child Jesus, who lived in France in the late 1800's, struggled to discover, to learn, her special vocation in the Church. She describes this search in her autobiography.

She prayed and read St. Paul's First Letter to the Corinthians. The Church has a variety of members who develop their expertise for the glory of God. Theresa did not recognize herself in any of the members or ministries Paul described. Finally, it came to her.

"I saw and realized that love sets off the bounds of all vocations, that love is every-

5

thing, that this same love embraces every time and place. In one word, that love is everlasting.

"Then, nearly ecstatic with supreme joy in my soul, I proclaimed: O Jesus, my love, at last I have found my calling: my call is to love."

This book of prayers speaks directly to God, Who is all loving and deserving of all our love. St. John tells us, "God is love, and whoever abides in love, abides in God, and God in him" (1 Jn 4:16).

The prayers, one for each day in the year, focus on God's love and our response in the loving relationship. With God's grace, hopefully, the loving relationship will grow deeper and stronger as time goes by.

HOEVER wishes to come after Me must deny self, take up the cross, and follow Me. —Lk 9:23

Loving God More

Lord, You are very clear in Your commandments. The first and most important command is to love You. This calls for complete giving, a loving response, with my whole heart and soul. I wish it were so in my case. I struggle with myself every step of the way. How can I turn myself inside out so there is nothing held back?

Only You, Lord, are limitlessly lovable. It is almost beyond comprehension, yet my shallow mind seems to grasp the concept. I love You, Lord. Help me to obey You more.

ET us therefore love, because God first loved us.

—1 Jn 4:19

Expressions of Love

Let everything that I do today be an expression of love. You, Lord, are my greatest blessing. You brought me into existence. You sheltered me in my mother's womb. I am nourished with the fruit of Your land. You enlighten me about Yourself. You are my Creator. Thank You for the gift of life.

You brought us into existence. You continue to love us. Our lives are filled with light and joy. Move us to hold back nothing in loving You. May every thought, word, and deed be a declaration of my love, consecrating all life's details to Your glory. I love You, Lord.

LTHOUGH I walk in the valley of the shadow of death, I will fear no evil for You are with me.

—Ps 23:4

Ups and Downs

When things go bad, Lord, when life's difficulties mount up, it is time to say, I love You. Let me see through setbacks. You do not stop loving me when I feel miserable. There are times when dark clouds hover overhead and confusion enters my soul. You are never far away. Your love does not take a holiday.

To be mindful of Your grace brings comfort. Help me to love You more because You are working out my eternal salvation in mysterious ways. I love You, Lord.

 NE thing I ask of the Lord; this I seek: to dwell in the house of the Lord all the days of my life.

—Ps 27:4

Never Too Late

It is never too late to love You, Lord. As life progresses we often go off in other directions. We love ourselves instead of You. We seem to forget what life is all about. Yet no one and nothing is more deserving of love than You, Lord.

Why does it take so much time for this to sink in? It is like rain water gradually seeping into the ground. There are rocky surfaces, too. Many Saints, like Augustine, needed time to grow in their appreciation. Capacity to love does increase. I love You, Lord.

OR those who love God, all things work together unto good.

—Rom 8:28

Unfathomable Love

Sometimes I become angry, Lord, when I cannot have my way. But, after quiet thought and prayer, I realize that Your thinking is better than mine. You know best. How limited is my perspective! You love me beyond my wildest expectations and dreams.

Your love is included in all that happens and permeates our world. It is unfathomable. Embracing Your holy will brings peace to mind and heart. All other alternatives fall short. In sickness and in health, I love You, Lord.

 OOK at the birds of the air: they do not sow or reap or gather into barns; yet your heavenly Father feeds them.

—Mt 7:26

Secure in God's Love

Love is my calling, my vocation. It is a life-long quest and the challenge of a lifetime. Nevertheless, love requires me to place others first. Love is not love until it is given away. Where is the security? Who will provide? Fear makes for hesitation.

Jesus encourages us to depend on You, Lord. Because You are all-loving, You provide for everyone. You teach us to love. Love makes the world go round smoothly. When we care, we share. The lesson of love is indispensable. I love You, Lord.

OVE is patient and is kind; it is not jealous, not puffed up.

—1 Cor 13:14

Not Jealous

The Scriptures speak of You, Lord, as a "jealous God." It is a manner of speaking. You are the epitome of love. Of course, there are jealous people. They live in fear, They perceive danger in relationships. Confidence and trust are missing.

But You, Lord, are all good and deserving of all our love. We go astray when You are not first in our lives. True love is not jealous. I love You, Lord.

 ONSIDER it joy when you fall into various trials knowing that the testing of your faith begets perseverance.

—Jas 1:2-3

Fit To Be Tied

I love You, Lord. When I am frustrated and "fit to be tied," it is not because You do not love me. You love me through the process of purification. Frustration is included in the refinement. We are not born perfect. Through Your gift of grace, we attempt to overcome our shortcomings.

You love us despite our sins. You know conversion is possible. When our spirits are low, and we are dissatisfied with ourselves, Your love sustains us. I love You, Lord.

EYE has not seen or ear heard, nor has it entered the heart of man, what God has prepared for those who love Him.

—1 Cor 2:9

In God Alone

The Psalmist declares that You, Lord, are our God and our happiness lies in You, alone. Ultimate contentment comes when we are face to face with You. Philosophy defines happiness as "the stable and perfect possession of the highest good." This has to be heaven.

We look forward to being with You. What delights us now, is but a reflection of what will come. How beautifully this anticipation flavors our life and brightens our vision! I love You, Lord.

I LOVE You, O Lord, my strength; O Lord, my rock, my stronghold, and my deliverer.

—Ps 18:2-3

With Words

Lord, three little words, "I love you," have great impact. Everyone wants to hear them. Husbands and wives reassure one another many times a day. Parents express their love to their children. Shakespeare wrote, "Words without thought never to heaven go."

You look into our souls. Sincerity is the blessing of our interior sentiments. Our relationship develops only through love. And You, Lord, have loved us from the instant of creation. I love You, Lord.

GOD so loved the world that He gave His only Son, that those who believe in Him may have eternal life.

—Jn 3:16-17

JAN. 11

No Greater Love

Heavenly Father You so loved all of us that You sent Your Son. The fullness of Your love is Jesus Christ. Greater love for us cannot be shown than that which Jesus expressed. He laid down His life for our salvation. The crucifix stands as the ultimate symbol of Your love. How can we begin to comprehend the magnitude of this sacrifice!

Quicken our minds, Lord, and penetrate our hearts with Your grace. When the impact of Your love touches us, our souls are transformed. I love You, Lord. Draw me closer.

AS the deer longs for streams of water, my soul longs for You, O God.

—Ps 42:2

JAN. 12

Over and Over Again

Only in loving You, Lord, will I find delight in Your presence. You have shown us the way to happiness in the Scriptures. The Psalmist writes, "My soul thirsts for God, the living God; when shall I come and behold the face of God?" (Ps. 42:3).

The message is clear, page after page. It is good to repeat this many times a day. Singleness of purpose is not to be compromised. All other details of life fall into place when my love is complete. I love You, Lord.

NOT everyone who says to Me, "Lord, Lord" shall enter the kingdom of heaven; only the one who does the will of My Father in heaven.—Mt 7:21

Rising Above

Lord, if You never answer another one of my prayers, it will not matter. Your holy will is superior to all my desires. You know what is best for me. My love must never be conditioned by Your answers.

There comes a time to get beyond my own will, my own needs, my own pleasures. The challenge is to rise above them and to enjoy the embrace of Your tremendous love. Accepting Your holy will is accepting You, my loving Lord. I love You, Lord.

LET the thought of God be in your mind and all your discourse on the commandments.

—Sir 9:23 (Vulgate)

Even My Thoughts

Lord, consciousness is a blessing after Your own image and likeness. The human mind is a gift, free and spontaneous. Still You provide the food for thought. How can I have ideas if You do not inspire me?

I am at liberty to think as I wish. Good thoughts or bad thoughts? We can entertain the high-minded and noble. We can choose the base and the evil. Wisdom teaches that even my innermost spirit is unwittingly favored. You share Your beauty and truth in freedom. I love You, Lord.

ET us enter into His presence with praises; with songs let us glorify Him.

—Ps 95:2

JAN. 15

In God's Loving Presence

Lord, some Saints spend hours in meditation. They are in touch with You. Prayer is a delight. These men and women seem so otherworldly. My attention span is much more limited. After a few minutes I run out of words.

I do realize that, even without words, there is comfort and contentment sitting in church before the tabernacle where Jesus dwells. How blest we are in Your loving presence! I love You, Lord.

N praying, do not multiply words, as the Gentiles do; for they think that by saying a great deal, they will be heard.

—Mt 6:7

JAN. 16

The Habit of Words

Lord, I find myself praying often with memorized prayers, Our Father's and Hail Mary's. After all, Jesus taught us how to pray the Our Father. The Hail Mary must cause Your mother to smile.

Many people prefer to pray spontaneously. Both forms of prayer, memorized and spontaneous, are acceptable. We are to ask so that we will receive. But if our communication is limited to the "gimmies," it is indeed limited. Praise You! Thank You! I love You, Lord.

HEY will go from virtue to virtue; they will see the God of gods in Zion.

—Ps 84:8

A Virtue

Lord, I know that habits happen through repetition. Practicing the piano for years makes for a musician. When our habits are good, they are called virtues. How good it is to have the habit of saying "I love You."

Our entire lives are to be spent in developing love to its perfection. Saying "I love You" renews my efforts. It reminds me how much I must try to live up to Your expectations. Love is centered in the human will. Fulfilling Your holy will is the only way. And where there is love, there is no labor. I love You, Lord.

 O You I lift up my soul, O Lord, my God. In You I place my trust.

—Ps 25:1-2

Perfect Love

Perfect love leaves no room for fear. Relationship with You must not depend on stress. Imperfect love is when I dread the loss of heaven and the pains of hell. Just as the father of a family wants his children to love him rather than fear him, so it is with You.

The Psalmist does say that fear of the Lord is the beginning of wisdom, but it is merely a beginning. There has to be growth in trust and confidence. May our relationship grow each day. I love You, Lord.

THE Lord is my light and my salvation: whom shall I fear?

—Ps 27:1

Light in the Darkness

Lord, one day Jesus told the story of a Prodigal Son, who squandered his inheritance on wine, women, and song. But his father continued to love him. Eventually, the son came to his senses and returned home, repentant and forlorn. Then his father threw his arms around him, and welcomed him.

Mothers and fathers continue to love their wayward sons and daughters. Sin does merit punishment. But Your mercy and forgiveness is given lovingly to all who repent. You light up my life though I walk in the valley of darkness. I love You, Lord.

I WILL give thanks to the Lord with my mouth, and in the midst of the multitude I will praise Him. —Ps 109:30

My Gift

There is a radio announcer who reminds his listeners that each new day is a gift. Everyone is free to make whatever he wishes with the blessed time. Lord, let everything I do be pleasing in Your sight.

The day is filled with Your gifts. Make me more aware of Your favors that I may love You more. St. John says, "God is love" (1 Jn 4:8). For all my gifts and Your love, thank You. I love You, Lord.

THE Lord will give you rest and you shall be like a watered garden.
—Isa 58:11

Love Is Like Life

Life is like a garden, Lord. It has to be cultivated. Farmers plant the seeds, then fertilize and weed, and they pray for rain.

Living relationships, too, call for cultivation. Jesus Christ, Who is "the Way, and the Truth, and the Life" (Jn 14:6), defines the path of life. Loving You, Lord, with our whole heart and soul, and loving our neighbor as ourselves, summarizes all Your commandments. Our relationship is alive. It matures graciously in the sunshine. You give us life and love. I love You, Lord.

WE have received not the spirit of the world, but the Spirit that is from God, that we may know the things given us by God. —1 Cor 2:12

The Totality of God

There are snatches of happiness in life. We experience small delights day after day. Sometimes we reward ourselves after diligent labor. Maybe we eat a sweetmeat after dieting. Old friends get together on occasion to reminisce about how wonderful it used to be.

Lord, whatever is included in our notions about happiness—health, wealth, security—all the blessings of life have their origin in You. The totality of good things is from You. I love You, Lord. Thank You for everything.

UT as for you, the very hairs of your head are numbered.

—Mt 10:30

I Am Special

Parents carry photos of their children. They like to think that their sons and daughters are special. And they are!

Lord, there may be billions of people on the face of the earth, but each one of us is special to You. We feel this way. And it is true. None of us is unnoticed. All of us are loved. Heavenly Father, all of our photos are in Your wallet. I love You, Lord.

 HEY cried to the Lord and He delivered them. He stilled the storm to a gentle breeze and the waves became quiet.

—Ps 107:28-29

Calm during Storms

The lyrics of a song declare, "You'll never walk alone." We are always in Your presence, Lord. There are storms that lash out as we sail through life. The Apostles experienced this first hand on the Sea of Galilee. Jesus was asleep. They woke Him. And He raised His hands and calmed the wind and the waves.

When calamities creep into our lives, when crises challenge our tranquility, our faith in You sustains us. Crosses may not disappear, but You strengthen us to carry them. I love You, Lord.

VEN if you suffer for justice' sake blessed are you. Do not be afraid.

—1 Pet 3:14

Carrying Our Crosses

Jesus never said that life would be a picnic. He did say that no one could be His follower unless he carried his cross. Lord, we know Christ cannot be separated from His Cross. His crucifixion is the ultimate sacrifice in reparation for all sins.

Saints identified with Christ in their sufferings. They welcomed trials, not because they were sadistic, but because they were realistic. You have shown us the way. I love You, Lord.

 ESUS said to him, "I am the Way, and the Truth, and the Life. No one comes to the Father except through Me." —Jn 14:6

The Way to Eternity

Jesus spoke about everlasting life on many occasions. People were concerned and curious. Lord, there seems to be less interest today. It would appear that many think that death ends everything. Not so! Christ's resurrection from the tomb provides believers with certainty and security.

One of Christ's great miracles was calling Lazarus back to life several days after his demise. The Gospel says that many people came to believe in Jesus after this stunning event. I love You, Lord.

THE heavens tell the glory of God, and the firmament proclaims the work of His hands. —Ps 19:2

Acclaiming God's Love

Love tends to diffuse itself. Lord, love is not all boxed up and stagnant. It is active. It reaches out just as God reached out beyond Himself to create the world. Everything that we see and experience has God's label of love on it.

The birds and the fish, the mountains and the hills, the rushing streams and roaring seas, all bear witness to God's love. Since humans are fashioned after Your own image and likeness it is our delight to praise and to thank You clearly and consciously. I love You, Lord.

IN the person who keeps His word, the love of God is truly perfected. —1 Jn 2:5

JAN. 28

Reaching Perfection

When a baseball pitcher retires all the batters on the opposing team without one reaching first base, they call it a perfect game. Lord, many people strive for perfection in music, in sports, in physical fitness, and more. Most men and women do not talk about living perfect lives.

Our lifetime calling is to love You—in our worship, our association with others, and our fulfillment of responsibilities. Not to love You is to render life meaningless. You set before us life and death. Help us to choose life. I love You, Lord.

ELIGHT in the Lord, and He will give you what you desire.

—Ps 37:4

Delight in Loving

Lord, once a priest told a story about cat food promoted in great style that sold well at the start, but then sales dwindled. Why? The cats didn't like it. Then he said this is probably why some people do not go to church. They just don't like it. Perhaps the liturgies leave much to be desired.

Human nature does have its resistance to Your holy will. But the alternative of not having a loving relationship with You is a hell of a situation. Loving You is a delight. I love You, Lord.

 OU are near, O Lord, and all Your commandments are steadfast.

—Ps 119:151

The Nearness of God

"From a distance, God is watching"—song lyrics, pleasant, but perhaps, theologically inaccurate. There is no distance, Lord. You hear our prayers without delay. You know the past, present, and future at a glance. Our perception, at times, however, places You far away. We speak to You in desperation, hoping that You will hear.

There is comfort in knowing that You are near. My soul is at peace. This is not an exercise in imagination. It is reality. I love You, Lord.

ESUS said, "My food is to do the will of Him Who sent Me."

—Jn 4:34

Welcoming God's Will

Lord, we are blessed when we receive both the bad and the good with equanimity of heart. This disposition conquers life. Without doubt, it is wisdom to accept everything that You send.

You always convey blessings. Since You are goodness itself, everything You do has to be good. We keep praying "Thy will be done." We have to believe it. And so all Your judgments and decisions are welcome. I love You, Lord. Thank You.

IVE thanks to the Lord for He is good; His mercy endures forever.

—Ps 118:1

FEB. 1

The Ultimate Good

Lord, after creation, You stepped back and saw that everything was good. Genesis describes it this way. Whatever is fashioned by Your hand is unmistakably perfect. We pursue many created blessings. Some people attempt to embrace wealth and find security.

No one carries material possessions from this world to the next. All our acquisitions totaled cannot equal You, Yourself, Lord. Lead us from the temptation of valuing objects more than You. I love You, Lord.

ET each one give . . . not grudgingly, . . . for God loves a cheerful giver.

— 2 Cor 9:7

Better To Give

Jesus said He came to serve, not to be served. Lord, our love for You is reflected in the service we extend to our brothers and sisters. What we do for others is done for You. You take our assistance personally. This tells us how close our relationship is to You.

Christ declared it is better to give than to receive. Peace and satisfaction is our reward for loving those that You love. Our opportunities are limitless. I love You, Lord, and all those that You love.

 UST as a father has compassion on his children, the Lord has compassion on those who fear Him.

— Ps 103:13

Patient and Compassionate

Lord, You wait for us patiently to discover our mistakes. You are patient and compassionate. St. Peter tells us, "The Lord is long-suffering with you, not wishing that any should perish but that all should turn to repentance" (2 Pet 3:9). You allow us to act freely although we defy Your holy will.

You see our potential. In time it may be our own misery that moves us to turn around. Your love wins our hearts. You do not abandon us. I love You, Lord.

TO You I lift up my eyes, to You enthroned in heaven.

— Ps 123:1

Our Eyes Are on the Lord

Lord, no matter what happens we need to keep focused. Sickness and disease strike. Earthquakes and floods devastate. How can this happen in the presence of a loving God?

The mystery of suffering continues from age to age. But in Your Divine Providence You right all wrongs. Our vision is blurred. Jesus showed us the way by carrying His Cross. In good times and in bad times we must keep our eyes on You. I love You, Lord.

WORTHY are You, O Lord, our God, to receive glory and honor and power.

— Rev 4:11

All Glory and Honor

During the Holy Sacrifice of the Mass the priest holds the Eucharist high and proclaims, "Through Him, and with Him, and in Him, O God, almighty Father, in the unity of the Holy Spirit, all glory and honor is Yours, for ever and ever." It is through Christ that we properly acknowledge You, Lord.

The people in the pews respond with a resounding "Amen." They call this the "Great Amen." Our minds and our hearts are correctly aligned if we learn this lesson. I love You, Lord.

I WILL bless the Lord at all times; His praise shall be always on my lips.

— Ps 34:2

Proclaiming the Truth

Some truths, Lord, are more important than others. Your love for all of us is the greatest truth. This calls for joyful singing. Once this is appreciated, our lives are changed.

We begin to relate to You eagerly. We wish to please You. We are mindful of Your presence and we are not uncomfortable. You have so loved us all that You sent Your Son, Jesus. Our lives become a proclamation of our religious convictions. I love You, Lord.

 MANY other signs Jesus worked in the sight of His disciples, which are not written in this book.

— Jn 20:30

Countless Signs

Jesus set forth many signs to win the hearts of people. We call them miracles, Lord. The blind saw, the lame walked, and the lepers were cleansed. These wonderful happenings demonstrated His Divinity. Many began to believe in Jesus after Lazarus came forth from the tomb.

Jesus' greatest sign was rising from the dead, His resurrection. All of these things provide a basis for our belief. The signs make Your love perfectly clear. I love You, Lord.

AY the Father of glory grant you wisdom . . . that you may know what is the hope of His calling.

— Eph 1:17-18

My Calling, My Quest, My Destiny

The one word, love, answers all three questions about calling, quest, and destiny. Your grace enlightens me, Lord. For centuries these answers have been written clearly on each page of the Scriptures.

Anything less than loving You with my whole heart and soul falls short of the goal of life. Love is gauged on how much we do for others. Does life have a purpose? It certainly does. I love You, Lord.

SEEK not My own will, but the will of Him Who sent Me.

— Jn 5:30

God's Will Articulated

Jesus spells out our relationship with You, heavenly Father. He says that Your will takes priority. When the disciples asked Him how to pray, He taught them the Our Father. "Thy will be done," Jesus declares.

Worship, reverence for Your name, keeping holy the Sabbath Day, honor for parents, purity and chastity, honesty, and respect for life—all should be an integral part of everyone's life. I love You, Lord. I cherish Your will.

EVEN if my father and mother should forsake me, the Lord will still receive me.
—Ps 27:10

Steadfast Love

People fall in love and fall out again. Lord, You never fall out of love. Your love is steadfast. I pray that my love for You may be persevering.

They say that love is blind. Relationships begun sincerely are torn apart in time. Marriages go on the rocks, families become unstable and devastated. Send Your grace to keep our hearts forever in harmony with Yours. Bless all those whose lives have become unsettled. May they see all things in the light of eternity. I love You, Lord.

I HAVE loved you with an everlasting love; therefore, I have taken pity on you.
— Jer 31:3

Enduring Love

Temptation happens, Lord. Reality tells us that the loving relationship we have with You is subject to temptation. The devil whispers, "There is happiness in sin."

We are weak, but Your grace is sufficient for us. We have a choice. We must keep our eyes on the goal. Freedom is not freedom if it defies Your authority. Your love is enduring, Lord. Strengthen us so that our love will be enduring. I love You, Lord.

ESUS said, "If anyone loves Me, he will keep My words, and My Father will love him, and We will come to him.

FEB.
12

—Jn 14:23

Three Little Words

There is a song with the title "Three Little Words." The words are "I love you." Is there any other phrase spoken more frequently? Lord, You, too, delight in these words. With these words husbands and wives reassure one another, sweethearts confirm their sentiments, parents comfort their children.

At Baptism, we make this serious declaration to love You as Christians, followers of Your Son. Loving You is not a difficult choice. It is the only choice. I love You, Lord.

 E may say with confidence: "The Lord is my helper. I will not be afraid." —Heb 13:6

FEB.
13

Confidence

Lord, Your decisions are always right. Your judgments are always true. There are no mistakes. You cannot deceive, nor can You be deceived. That is because You are all knowing and all loving. We have a guarantee that cannot be matched.

As we journey through life there are shadows and fears. But You have sent Your Son, Lord. Jesus is the Light of the World. We have only to think of Your love, heavenly Father. The cold frost of doubt dissolves in the bright sunshine. I love You, Lord.

THE ways of God are perfect, the word of the Lord is proved by fire.
— Ps 18:31

God's Ways Are Perfect

Wisdom radiates through the psalms, songs of praise. Lord, as limited as humans are, we have some concept that You are God, magnificent, and awesome.

When You say something, it is absolute truth. It is a sure guide, never to be doubted. We should read the Bible prayerfully. There is a need for authoritative interpretation—Your living voice exercised in the Church. We learn from You. You speak the language of love. And I love You, too, Lord.

OU who abide in the shadow of the Almighty, say to the Lord, "My refuge and fortress, my God in Whom I trust."
— Ps 91:1-2

Abiding in God

Praying out of love puts us in touch with You, Lord. There are times when I fly to You in desperation. Pain and suffering brings me to my knees. But I want to pray simply out of love.

You love me. This realization is overwhelming. You are the source and epitome of love. No person, place, or thing compares with You, Lord. To see clearly, to comprehend, is a blessing. To arrive at this perfect state of mind and soul calls for Your grace. I love You, Lord.

FOR love is strong as death, devotion relentless as the netherworld; its flames are a blazing fire.

—Song 8:6B

Living for Love

"I wanna be loved by you, just you—" lyrics from a vintage song. Lord, although the words are directed toward lovers and sweethearts, all of us live for love. We seek love from infancy to old age. Generally speaking, life is considered a bust if we are unlucky in love. But we are really in trouble if we have not come to love You first and totally.

Life is worth living if we live it loving You. You have created us for the very purpose of loving us forever. Mindful of Your love we are lifted in spirit. I love You, Lord.

BLESSED are you when men insult you and persecute you . . . for My sake. Your reward will be great in heaven.

—Mt 5:11-12

Blessed in Martyrdom

The first three centuries of the Church are called the Age of Martyrs. Followers of Christ were tortured, thrown to the wild beasts in the arena, and crucified by the Romans.

Lord, their pains and distress were not because You withdrew Your love. Just as through His Cross Jesus redeemed the world, so do our individual sufferings find merit. The Martyrs were privileged to demonstrate heroic virtue. I love You, Lord.

LOVE the Lord, you faithful. The Lord looks after the loyal.

— Ps 31:24

FEB. 18

Unconditional Love

Your love, Lord, is unconditional. It does not depend on anyone's response. If no one returns Your love, You continue to love. You are love itself. Love does not have ulterior motives.

My love for You must not be conditioned on Your response to my prayers. Whatever You decide is blessing for me. I need to learn how to love. It is sound perspective to love You simply and solely because You are my God. I love You, Lord.

IVE as free men, yet not using your freedom as a cloak for evil, but as servants of God.

— 1 Pet 2:16

FEB. 19

Freedom To Love

Lord, You do not compel us to love You. You win our hearts with Your unspeakable love. We are free. We make our own choices. This gift comes with human nature, created after Your image and likeness.

Pure love, complete unselfishness, is a lifetime goal. St. John reminds us, "He who loves God should love his brothers also" (1 Jn 4:21). If I should die today, let me die as a loving person. It is the only way into Your Divine presence. I love You, Lord.

E can expect to live seventy years, or maybe eighty, if we are healthy. . . . Then suddenly our time is up and we disappear. —Ps 90:10

Glory to God

"The path of glory leads but to the grave," the poet tells us, Lord. A visit to the cemetery, a walk among the tombstones, brings sobering thoughts. They remind us that we are all mortal.

We have a span of years to recognize You, Lord, and to respond to You. We can see the futility of trying to attain glory for ourselves. We are blessed when we are meek and humble of heart. Glory be to God, now and forever. I love You, Lord.

HE grass is withered, and the flower is fallen; but the word of our Lord endures forever. — Isa 40:8

God's Word

Jesus read the Bible. Once in the synagogue on the Sabbath, He read from the Prophet Isaiah about the Messiah. Jesus declared, "Today this Scripture has been fulfilled in your hearing" (Lk 4:21).

He was drawing from Your word, Lord, and pointing out that He was Himself the Messiah. Your word is sacred, completely accurate, and absolutely true. Accepting Your word is accepting You. Your love is written on each page of the Bible. Inspire us to embrace Your word. I love You, Lord.

DO not join faith in our glorious Lord Jesus Christ with partiality toward persons.
—Jas 2:1

Esteeming Every Person

It is easier getting along with people when we realize that You love them, Lord. Everyone is included in Your love—the pleasant and the obnoxious, the stranger and the neighbor, even our enemies. Your Son, Jesus came for the salvation of all.

We are invited to see the young and the old, the rich and the poor, as You see them. Change and reform is possible for all of us. Enlighten us with Your perspective. I love You, Lord.

LET us love not in word or speech but in deed and truth.
—1 Jn 3:18

The Sweetest Phrases

Poets and song writers wax eloquent with lyrics about love. They pen lines that lovers find expressive and appropriate. But there are not enough words in any language to articulate accurately the love You deserve, Lord.

Consequently, we borrow a line, "So take the sweetest phrases the world has ever known and make believe I said them all to You." Thinking of You, Lord, our efforts will always come up short. We can only offer You the sincerity of our hearts. I love You, Lord.

TEACH me to do Your will, because You are my God.

— Ps 143:10

Accepting Vicissitudes Graciously

There will come a time when accepting Your holy will, Lord, is the only thing to do—that is, if we want interior peace. We should welcome Your will, embrace it eagerly. When life seems to deal devastating blows to us, accepting vicissitudes graciously is the only way to go.

You watch over the birds of the air and the lilies of the field. Your constant care exceeds all our expectations. You are a loving God. This, too, is Your nature, Your Divine nature. You see things far beyond our sight. There is never an unloving gesture. I love You, Lord.

MAY we rejoice in your victory and in the name of our God raise banners; may the Lord fulfill all your petitions.

— Ps 20:6

Perfect Fulfillment

We can become many things in life, Lord. And we can attain many too, but they are meaningless without loving You. Our souls are empty unless we love You.

When we come to lifetime's exclusive goal of loving You, there is perfect fulfillment. St. Paul says, "If I give away all my goods to the poor, and deliver my body over so that I may boast, yet do not have love, I am nothing" (1 Cor 13:3). We are everything with love because we are with You, Lord. I love You, Lord.

ERVE the Lord with gladness; come into His presence with joy.

—Ps 99:2

Conscious of God

Nothing happens by chance. It appears, Lord, from time to time, that there are chance happenings. But the past, present, and future are Yours at a glance. You will everything into existence.

Each person that lives owes their totality to You, especially their consciousness. Jesus tells us about You: "He who sees Me sees also the Father" (Jn 14:9). You are always present and accessible. We have a true interpersonal relationship. You communicate, and your message is love. I love You, Lord.

UT you, brother, do not grow weary of doing good.

—2 Thes 3:13

Never Grow Weary

Who ever grows tired of hearing "I love you"? The message is expressed in thousands of ways. You, Lord, have communicated Your love throughout history. You guided Your chosen people through troubled waters.

There was sin and defiance. People learned of Your mercy and forgiveness. You promised a Messiah and deliverance and sent Jesus, Your Son. You, Lord, have not wearied in demonstrating Your love. Enlighten every heart to respond. I love You, Lord.

ET our sacrifice be made in Your sight this day . . . for there is no confusion to those who trust in You.

— Dan 3:40

Tangled

Sometimes we become tangled in our own emotions, Lord. We do not know how to extricate ourselves. It may have been an impulsive action, a spontaneous gesture, too quick a response. How we arrived at this disquieted state does not matter so much as regaining peace and equanimity.

This is a time of trial, an opportunity to persevere in patience. But You understand, heavenly Father, and You love us. Embrace us again and banish our confusion. I love You, Lord.

HAT is man, that You are mindful of him, or the son of man that You care for him?

— Ps 8:5

Purpose of Life

Many people wonder about the purpose of life. Why are we here? Where are we going? They fail to realize, Lord, that You are our origin and destiny.

They fail to see what a blessing life really is. And that it was out of love that You created us. All powerful, compelled by no one, You willed that there would be creatures after Your image and likeness. And so we are intelligent and free. Most of all, we are capable of loving. Seeking to respond to Your love by doing what You will makes the purpose of life true joy. I love You, Lord.

E said to them, "Why are you fearful? Are you still without faith?"
— Mk 4:40

Trust versus Fear

Trust comes with difficulty, Lord, when our feet are buried in quicksand. Fear envelops our innards. We are tempted to reach for alcohol or drugs, anything to soothe the clawing, savage feeling.

What does it take to quiet a tortured soul? Jesus said: "Do not be afraid; only have faith" (Mk 5:36). We must reach out and take Jesus' hand. Even trouble has its purpose. It leads to prayer. We are once again reunited with You. There is always hope. I love You, Lord.

ECEIVE the Holy Spirit; whose sins you shall forgive, they are forgiven them.
— Jn 20:22-23

Forgiveness

Your love is present in forgiveness, Lord. We kneel in the confessional, ridden with shame and guilt. You lift the burden from our shoulders, and the weight of sin disappears.

The priest, empowered by Christ, absolves our souls. Jesus, Who offered Himself on Calvary's cross, extends pardon and peace through the holy Sacrament: "Whose sins you forgive, they are forgiven" (Jn 20:23). Jesus came to call sinners, not the just. How consoling! I love You, Lord.

LL these blessings shall come upon
you if you hear His precepts.

**MAR.
3**

— Deut 28:2

Blessings

"I have said my prayers. What is God going
to give me?" a child asked. "Everything you
have is a gift from God!" her guardian replied.
Lord, You overwhelm us with graces and favors. How enlightened we are to see Your
love, which is so clear and apparent.

It gratifies us when others appreciate our
gifts. Heads of state, kings, even popes, exchange objects. Gifts are harbingers of good
cheer. Each day is a carefully wrapped pack-
age from You, Lord. We rejoice. I love You,
Lord.

F we sin, we are Yours, knowing Your
greatness, and if we sin not, we know that
we belong to You.

**MAR.
4**

— Wis 15:2

Knowing God

An epitaph on an old tombstone reads,
"Here lies the atheist John Doe. All dressed
up and no place to go." How destitute the person, Lord, who has little or no relationship
with You! How empty life must be for those
whose vision is limited to this world!

Why is it that religious men and women acknowledge You and others are without the
knowledge of the one, true God? Lord of love,
You provide the enlightenment and grace we
need. Help us to keep the flame of faith alive.
I love You, Lord.

THE fear of the Lord is pure, enduring forever; the judgments of the Lord are true, and all are just.

MAR. 5

— Ps 19:10

His Ways Are True

There is an Easter antiphon, Lord, that reads: "Give honor and praise to our God; all that He does is perfect and all His ways are true, alleluia." It is much easier serving You when we are convinced that Your ways cannot be improved upon.

Children have loving parents who only want them to be happy. They find security in the family. We, too, Your sons and daughters, find love and comfort in our family of faith. I love You, Lord.

BY the grace of God I am what I am, and His grace in me has not been fruitless.

MAR. 6

— 1 Cor 15:10

By Your Grace

A priest celebrating his fiftieth anniversary of ordination received praise and congratulations. He told a story about Jesus entering Jerusalem triumphantly riding on a beast of burden. Referring to the animal, the jubilarian said, "The poor ass thought the applause was for him."

By Your grace, Lord, we are what we are. There is nothing we have not received from You. Our calling is to praise You and it should flow effortlessly. We are privileged to serve, and we serve at Your pleasure. I love You, Lord.

IVE joy to the soul of Your servant, for to You I lift up my soul.

— Ps 86:4

The Joy of My Soul

We witness many people jumping for joy, Lord, when they win large amounts of money. Some exclaim, "Thank You, Jesus!" They attribute their blessings to Your bounty.

The Prophet Isaiah knew where his treasure was hidden. He cried out, "I will greatly rejoice in the Lord" (Isa 61:10) in thanksgiving for salvation and justice. Our complete uncompromised contentment, Lord, lies in You alone. I love You, Lord.

 REATER love than this no one has, that one lay down his life for his friends.

— Jn 15:13

Contemplating the Cross

The great theologian St. Thomas Aquinas said he learned more at the foot of the crucifix than from any other source. Lord, meditating on Jesus and His sacrifice, impresses us with His love. The Cross is a symbol of unspeakable love.

Each time we make the Sign of the Cross is an occasion to grow in appreciation. We trace the Cross on our forehead and shoulders identifying ourselves with Christ. The Cross stands as the key to heaven. In Baptism we die with Christ only to rise with Him. I love You, Lord.

IS heart shall be as hard as a stone, and as firm as a smith's anvil.

— Job 41:15

MAR. 9

With a Firm Heart

We cannot foresee the eventualities of life, Lord. Surprises lie around the corner of our many tomorrows. They say we are not tested beyond our strength. Your grace is sufficient for us.

We must be steadfast in our convictions and look to You for strength. You are at my side. This is not just wishful thinking. It is the truth. What is this like? It is like never doubting a loyal Friend Who is almighty. I love You, Lord.

————————

F you have risen with Christ, seek what pertains to higher realms, where Christ is seated at the right hand of God.

— Col 3:1

MAR. 10

Higher Realms

"What would you like to be when you grow up?" Is there any child who has not been asked this question? Lord, many young people coast along for years undecided. Has anyone ever stated the desire to be a Saint?

St. Paul admonishes that we set our heart on what pertains to higher realms where Christ is. Christians have perfection as the ultimate goal of life. Everyone has to be on the honor roll. Anything less is unthinkable. I love You, Lord.

41

OW can he who does not love his brother, whom he sees, love God, Whom he does not see? — 1 Jn 4:20

In All Circumstances

Lord, Your call to holiness and to a life of love applies to everyone everywhere. No one is excused. No one will be admitted to Your kingdom without first loving You totally.

Those who feel secure and sufficient often succumb to the temptation of ignoring You. Eternal life is not merely elusive without love—it is impossible. Our love for You extends to our neighbor. The young and the old, all have to be Good Samaritans. I love You, Lord.

BRAHAM believed, and it was credited to him as justice.

— Rom 4:3

Faith Recognizes God

Faith is a gift, freely given. It is a grace that You do not withhold from the sincere of heart. Some people have struggled to find You, Lord. Faith may be intangible, but it is real. It has You as its object, Lord.

Faith recognizes the truth of Your Divine presence in our world. The basis of our belief has its foundation in Your communication through the Prophets and holy leaders, but especially in Jesus, Your Son. It is possible to please You because of faith. I love You, Lord.

ET us love one another, for love is from God. And everyone who loves is born of God. **MAR.** — 1 Jn 4:7 **13**

Falling in Love

Love songs are full of words like "worship" and "adoration." There are zillions of films about people falling in love. This "falling" is frequently short-lived, alive one week and dead the next.

We pray that everyone eventually comes to loving You, Lord. All the love in the world derives from You as its Source. You are love. Only You are perfectly and limitlessly lovable. The goodness we perceive in others is first in You. I love You, Lord.

 ND Mary said, "My soul magnifies the Lord, and my spirit rejoices in God my Savior." **MAR.** — Lk 1:46-47 **14**

Mary

A poet described Jesus's mother as "our tainted nature's solitary boast." Everyone has original sin, except Mary. Conceived immaculately, she who figured so prominently in God's plan was born to Ann and Joachim.

By the power of the Holy Spirit Mary conceived and gave birth to Jesus. Her heart was in complete harmony with Your wishes. How blessed we are to have her prayerful intercession! I love You, Lord.

OU make my lamp shine, O Lord; my
God You enlighten my darkness.

— Ps 18:29

Enlightenment

Your grace opens the doors of understanding, Lord. They say we can know that You exist simply from reason. Philosophers set forth arguments that go from created matter back to the Creator.

Through the centuries, Lord, You reveal things about Yourself that go beyond rational ability. You send Jesus, Your Son, to teach us and the Holy Spirit to fire up our comprehension. It is easy to see that You have loved us first. I love You, Lord.

UT I, because of Your boundless mercy,
will enter Your house.

— Ps 5:8

Access to God's House

You have no office hours, Lord. We can speak to You day and night. You say, "My house is your house." How awesome that You take the time to listen to every person on the face of the earth!

It is plain to see that You have done everything possible for us to have a loving relationship. In times of trouble, You are near. On occasions of great rejoicing, You are present. Help us to always be mindful of Your presence. I love You, Lord.

VERY day is miserable for the oppressed, but a secure man enjoys a continual feast. — Prov 15:15

Strength and Security

Rocks signify security. The Rock of Gibraltar is a symbol of the indestructible, the secure. Lord, we try to cover all bases. We insure houses and cars and health. But there is only one policy that guarantees eternity.

The Psalmist tells us, "I love You, O Lord, my strength, O Lord, my rock, my stronghold, and my deliverer" (Ps 18:2-3). Heaven is attained by loving You, Lord. There has to be a reciprocation freely given to the overwhelming love that You have shown us. I love You, Lord.

 WILL ask the Father and He will give you another Advocate to abide with you forever. — Jn 14:16

Abiding in Love

Ecclesiastes teaches us wisdom: "The covetous man never has enough money, and the lover of wealth is never satisfied with his income; so this, too, is vanity" (Eccl 5:9). Vanity means that we are wasting our time.

Jesus said we are to seek first the Kingdom of God. This is true priority. Riches piled higher than mountains are nothing in comparison to Your love. Abiding in Your love is to abide in You. Children in the arms of their parents are content. You have made us Your sons and daughters. I love You, Lord.

NOT as man sees does God see; while man judges by appearance, the Lord sees into the heart.

— 1 Sam 16:7

Charm and Beauty

Cosmetics dress up the outside. Virtue adorns the heart. They say that beauty is only skin deep. Lord, You see right into our souls. While first impressions are important to people, Your comprehension envelops the total person.

"Charm is deceptive and beauty is vain, but a woman who fears the Lord is to be praised" (Prov 31:30). Tall people and short people, the young and the old, no matter their physical advantages, all are capable of loving You. Love is the deciding factor in gaining eternal life. I love You, Lord.

THE meek shall increase their joy in the Lord.

— Isa 29:19

Increased Appreciation

Lord, they say there is no standing still in the spiritual life. There should be advancement in virtue, character formation. There is struggle within, overcoming faults and failings, swimming against the tide.

Athletes engage in self-discipline for physical perfection. Those who love You strive for spiritual perfection, which cannot be attained in one or even several days. Nor is the journey all work and no play. Where there is love, there is no labor. Our appreciation for You increases. All is seen as a blessing. I love You, Lord.

E loved the Lord with his whole heart and daily sang His praises.

— Sir 47:8

MAR.
21

Singing God's Praises

Lord, St. Augustine suggests that people pray twice when they sing. Even this suggestion fails to move many in the church congregation. But we do hum and whistle and sing when we are happy.

Perhaps the renditions on Sunday morning are at times slow and somber. They are not toe tapping, that's for sure. When we are in love, the heart explodes with joy. Open all minds to recognize Your love. Each day and all it contains is a gift. I love You, Lord.

 ET your light shine before men so that they may see your good works and glorify your Father in heaven.

— Mt 5:16

MAR.
22

Statements

Unwittingly we make statements with action and inaction, with works and silence. Lord, there is no hiding our love. Followers of Your Son Jesus are not silent partners.

The early Christian martyrs made great statements by enduring torture and death. Wearing crucifixes and holy medals are declarations. Morality in the work place, the home, and the school counts. So does attendance at Mass. When we are in love we want the world to know it. I love You, Lord.

47

B E not conformed to this world but be transformed by the renewal of your mind that you may discern . . . the will of God.
— Rom 12:2

Counterculture

Lord, Jesus was countercultural. He preached a life-style different from the religious establishment of His day. His way was simple. It cut through the maze of legalistic requirements thought to be the norm of "religion." He urged His followers not to go along with the crowd.

Jesus predicted that the road would not be smooth. There would be trouble and persecution if they dared to identify with Him. I love You, Lord.

W HAT do you have that you have not received? And if you have received it, why do you boast as if you had not received it?
— 1 Cor 4:7

Never Outdone in Generosity

Lord, people play games like "Can You Top This?" Perhaps it's telling a tale about who caught the largest fish. Competition is strong in business as well as in sports and in life. When men and women vie with one another in kindness, everyone benefits.

Generosity makes everyone smile. You, Lord, are never outdone in blessings. There is nothing in life that we have not received from You. You have even sent Your Son Jesus for our salvation. I love You, Lord.

OR as the heavens are exalted above the earth, so are My ways exalted above your ways.
— Isa 55:9

As High as the Heavens

Your love for us, Lord, is beyond our comprehension. Once we come to understand and to appreciate this, our lives are changed. We relate to You in joy. There is Someone Who loves me. It is God.

"As the heavens tower over the earth, so God's love prevails over the faithful," the Psalmist says (Ps 103:11). The more I meditate on Your love, the stronger I am in meeting temptation. No one wants to hurt the one who loves them. I love You, Lord.

 EHOLD what manner of love the Father has bestowed upon us, that we should be called children of God.
— 1 Jn 3:1

Children of the Lord

If we have love, we have an identification. We are Your children, Lord. Jesus taught us to address You as "Our Father." You have begotten us, blessed us with life, given us being. Your only motive was love. Love tends to diffuse itself.

Let me live each day as a loving person. This is my true vocation. St. Francis expressed it clearly: "Where there is hatred, let me sow love. . . ." Jesus said we must always return good for evil. I love You, Lord.

E on your guard, stand fast in the faith, have courage, be strong.

— 1 Cor 16:13

**MAR.
27**

The Test of Faith

Without faith it is impossible to please You, Lord. But faith is constantly being put to the test. Our faith is in Jesus Christ Who is our Way, our Truth, and our Life. But it is not easy. Being a Christian calls for discipline and sacrifice.

Job, the Old Testament character who suffered so much, was taunted in his misery. No one wants to be miserable, but dedicated believers must be steadfastly loyal. I love You, Lord.

OUR thoughts should be directed to whatever is true, whatever is honorable, all that is holy, decent, worthy of praise.

— Phil 4:8

**MAR.
28**

Our Thoughts

Whatever is on paper was first in the mind, Lord. Writers think and then set their thoughts in print. Some creative authors elevate the mind. Others seem to exploit the darker side of life. Would that every word ever expressed by people reflected Your love!

Communication is a wonderful gift. You have communicated from the beginning of time to draw us closer to You. Inspire us, Lord, that we may sing Your praises. I love You, Lord.

NEW commandment I give you, that you love one another as I have loved you. — Jn 13:34

No Other Way

You show the way to happiness, Lord. Ever-lasting happiness is called heaven. It means living with You, Lord, for eternity. This ideal is gained by aligning ourselves with Your holy will. This is all summed up by one word, love.

We are to love You with every ounce of our strength. And we are to love those that You love, everybody. It is in seeking blessings for others that we are fulfilled. We spend a lifetime learning this lesson. I love You, Lord.

THERE is a time for everything. . . . A time to rend, and a time to sew; a time to keep silence, and a time to speak. — Eccl 3:1, 7

Time To Listen

Prayer is conversation, Lord, but it also includes listening. When we have completed our words, we remain quiet and still and receptive. You speak to us in the silence of our hearts. And there are times, too, when we cannot think of anything to say.

Prayerful exchange helps us to have rapport, Lord. Jesus instructs us to ask so that we will receive. But it is not always necessary to chat away. Longtime friends understand one another. I love You, Lord.

THE cares of the world and the deceit-
fulness of riches . . . choke the word
and make it fruitless.

— Mk 4:19

31

Cast Your Cares

Your shoulders are broad and strong, Lord.
St. Peter encourages us: "Cast all your anxiety
upon Him because He cares for you" (1 Pet
5:7). Jesus knows the troubles we have. His
experience was personal.

Jesus Who knew rejection opens His arms
in welcome. He says, "Come to Me, all you
who labor and are burdened. . . . For My yoke
is easy and My burden light" (Mt 11:28-30).
Your caring is expressed eloquently in Jesus'
caring. I love You, Lord.

FEAR the Lord, you holy ones, for there is
no want to those who fear Him.

— Ps 34:10

APR.

1

Wisdom

A sentence in the Psalms is quoted often,
Lord: "The fear of the Lord is the beginning of
wisdom" (Ps 111:10). When children are
growing up they both fear their parents and
love them. Even when they are afraid of being
punished, they still love their parents.

Everyone is wise to recognize that You are
God, our Creator, the Supreme Being. Awe,
respect, and reverence are in order. But the
believer who lingers in the state of fear, who
never graduates into love, does not live up to
Your expectations. I love You, Lord.

AM the living bread that has come down from heaven; whoever eats this bread shall live forever. — Jn 6:51

True Presence

You are truly present, Lord, throughout the universe. By Your knowledge and by Your power nothing escapes You. Your love touches everything in existence. In ancient times there was a special presence in the Ark of the Covenant, the sacred writings. Since Jesus came into the world there is a sacramental presence.

At the Last Supper Christ instituted the Eucharist. Today in thousands of churches there is a Divine Presence in tabernacles. We genuflect in reverence. We kneel quietly presenting our needs. We sit and meditate on this great privilege. I love You, Lord.

 APPY are the people whose God is the Lord. — Ps 144:15

Exact Expression

Lord, Jesus was precise in articulating Your holy will. He said the greatest commandment is to love You. If we come to love You to perfection, we will have accomplished the goal of life. There is no other great quest.

Poets speak about a "holy grail." They describe searches and crusades throughout the world. The explanation is much simpler. You are the Source of Good, Love Itself. You have created us for Yourself. You are our destiny. I love You, Lord.

H E gave him leave to go wherever he wished, with liberty to do what came to mind.   —Tob 1:14

APR. 4

Liberty in Loving

There is liberty in loving, Lord. Since You have said that we are to love You with our whole heart and soul, there have to be some side benefits. This almost sounds like a commercial. The giving of ourselves releases us.

Selfishness binds us. Your commandments tell us not to covet. It is in giving that we receive. Sharing is a way of life that cleanses us. The familiar Latin axiom *"Deus providebit!"* is a wonderful expression: "God will provide!" We are freed from the temptation to fear. I love You, Lord.

F OR this is the will of God, your sanctification.

— 1 Thes 4:3

APR. 5

Love! God's Will

Lord, praying for Your will is accepting Your love. You are love, and everything You do is loving. We avoid clashes of mind and heart when we embrace Your Divine Providence. You see beyond the horizon. Our view is limited.

There are some things in life that are out of our hands. We must accept them. That's wisdom and makes sense. If there is anything we should learn early in life it is that You love us with a tremendous love. I love You, Lord.

HEARD a loud voice of a great crowd in heaven saying, "Salvation and glory and power be to our God."

— Rev 19:1

APR. 6

Eternal Life

Lord, Your grace enlightens me. The purpose of life and the goal of life are made clear. You, Lord, are my destiny. Each year brings me closer to the ultimate reality, eternal life. Disposition of mind and heart is paramount.

They say, "Everybody wants to go to heaven, but nobody wants to die." It is both wrong and futile to try to escape Your holy will. Men, women, and children of all ages find happiness in Your loving presence. I love You, Lord.

RAISE the Lord, for He is good; God's love endures forever.

— Ps 136:1

APR. 7

God's Love Endures Forever

For centuries, Lord, people have been singing Your praises. This is fitting for each generation. "God's love endures forever" is the repeated line throughout Psalm 136. For all Your gifts of nature, the sun, the moon, and the stars, Lord, Your love endures.

Our relationship would be lopsided if we only prayed for blessings and needs. Of course, we turn to You in our trials. Praise and thanks are in order, too. Through all the challenges of life Your love sustains us. Your love is more apparent with each passing day. I love You, Lord.

E who loves Me will be loved by My Father, and I will love him and manifest Myself to him.

**APR.
8**

— Jn 14:21

Fusion with God

There may come a time, Lord, when our minds and hearts are in perfect harmony with Your holy will. We read about it in the lives of Saints. St. John Vianney teaches us, "Prayer is nothing else but union with God. God and the soul are fused together. . . ."

There has to be a mental and emotional state that can only be described as love. Our love, like that of the Saints, must be unconditional. Our love will never be like Yours, Lord, limitless, but it can be a total giving. I love You, Lord.

LL these died without receiving the promises . . . and acknowledging that they were pilgrims on earth.

**APR.
9**

— Heb 11:13

A Pilgrimage of Love

Lord, the bishops of the world described members of Christ's family of faith as a "pilgrim people." Their collective wisdom, reflected in the documents of Vatican Council II, speaks of Christians on a journey through life, a pilgrimage. Heaven is the ultimate shrine.

Pilgrimages are traditional. They provide occasion for something special in Your honor. There is repentance from sin and renewal of heart. Lord, may we walk hand in hand with You realizing how much You love us. We are on our way. I love You, Lord.

THE patient man shows much good sense, but the impatient man displays his folly.

— Prov. 14:29

Bearing Wrongs Patiently

To err is human, Lord, to forgive is Divine. It is an old axiom but still true today. There are times when folks expect more of us and they are disappointed. We pray that our bad example does not lead little ones astray.

It is reassuring, Lord, to remember that many sins are forgiven for those who love much. May those we serve bear our mistakes patiently. May they see through our feeble efforts and realize it is You, Lord, that is to be loved unreservedly. I love You, Lord.

LTHOUGH He should slay me, I will trust in Him.

— Job 13:15

Steadfast Trust

Habakkuk the Prophet was not easily discouraged, Lord. It must please You when believers trust steadfastly. Habakkuk says, "Though the flocks vanish from the fold and there be no herd in the barns, yet I will rejoice in the Lord" (3:17-18).

There are people who are optimists. They usually see the bright side of life. They are not blind to misfortune. But they see vicissitude as opportunity to learn and grow. Somehow this is what You must want us all to be, secure in Your love. I love You, Lord.

ET my prayer be as incense before You, the lifting up of my hands as the evening sacrifice.

APR. 12

— Ps 141:2

Prayer Channels the Heart

Most people in the United States pray, Lord. Surveys show the majority speak to You sometime. How we pray reveals how we feel about You, how we relate. Some may recite memorized prayers.

But You must also be delighted, Lord, when we talk to You from our hearts. Meditation, quiet exchange, and listening are all part of the communication. It is good to pray frequently because prayer directs the mind and channels the heart. I love You, Lord.

ROW in the grace and knowledge of our Lord and Savior, Jesus Christ.

APR. 13

— 2 Pet 3:18

Developing the Relationship

People talk about having a meaningful relationship, Lord. Young folks sizing up the prospects for marriage know that there is a "getting to know you" process—dating, picnics, learning likes and dislikes, whatever. Relationships have to develop and mature.

All this has to do with You, too, Lord. We read about Jesus, how You sent Him to our world for our happiness: "God so loved the world that He gave His only Son" (Jn 3:16). Hopefully it is clear that the relationship is characterized and defined by love. I love You, Lord.

JOHN answered and said, "He must increase, but I must decrease."

— Jn 3:27, 30

Christ Must Increase

Our faith is in Jesus Christ. Lord, Your Son is the one and only Mediator between heaven and earth. Jesus was clear when He said: "I am the Way, and the Truth, and the Life. No one comes to the Father except through Me" (Jn 14:6).

We have a Christ-centered religion. In Your great love, Lord, You sent Your Son. Strengthen us amid temptations that distract us from Christ and happiness with You. I love You, Lord.

SEEK first the kingdom of God and His justice, and all these things shall be given you besides.

— Mt 6:33

Seek First God's Kingdom

Lord, when people's lives are in good order, it is said that "they have it all together." There is peace and calm. The loose ends are all in place. Chances are that not all challenges and temptations are going to disappear.

But Saints demonstrated how to keep their balance in a topsy turvy world. You, Lord, figured prominently in everything that they did. They drew their direction and strength from You. All lives are well ordered if they are centered in You. I love You, Lord.

AY to day pours forth this word, night to night sends out this knowledge.
— Ps 19:3

16

Created in Love

"The heavens tell the glory of God; the skies proclaim the work of His hands" (Ps 19:2). Lord, everything that exists is the result of Your love. The sun, the moon, and the stars, are the product of Your creation. What You bring into being flows from Your love.

Sunsets, rainbows, colorful foliage, scenic views, all reflect Your handiwork. On occasion the beauty takes our breath away. We are enlightened. We marvel at Your goodness. The world is our playground. Thank You for our blessings. I love You, Lord.

HE mercy of the Lord is from eternity to eternity toward those who fear Him.
— Ps 103:17

APR.
17

Mercy

History tells of Your mercy, Lord. From the beginning of the world people dared to sin, to defy Your holy will. Time after time patiently and graciously You forgive. No one is as merciful as You, Lord.

But Jesus teaches us to forgive. How often? Seven times? No, seventy times seven times, or as much as is needed. We pray, "Forgive us our trespasses as we forgive those who trespass against us." Love has many expressions. One of the sweetest is Your compassion. I love You, Lord.

USBANDS, love your wives just as Christ loved the Church.

— Eph 5:25

Encouraged To Say "I Love You"

Marriage Encounter people are encouraged to say " I love you." Husbands and wives engage in a program geared to bring them closer together. They learn about one another, Lord, even though they may have been married for years.

Enlightenment is a special grace of the Holy Spirit. Of course, those three little words are not exclusive to spouses. They are appropriate for everyone. The words are like magic. They lift our spirits. But most of all they are to be addressed to You, Lord. I love You, Lord.

 HE word of the Lord is true; all His works are trustworthy.

— Ps 33:4

Love by Design

Many artists sign their works. Lord, all creation bears the sign of Your love. Both the animate and the inanimate reflect the loving stamp of Your hand. Even in freedom You guide and direct. Divine Providence has its way.

The Psalmist declares, "The plan of the Lord stands forever, wise designs through all ages" (Ps 33:11). By Your grace we have insight into history. How blessed and peaceful the person who experiences Your love in everything that occurs! I love You, Lord.

I N Him you too are being built together into a dwelling place for God in the Spirit.
— Eph 2:22

Changing

Lord, maturity calls for change. There is process from one stage of development to another. Progress presumes alteration. Pity the static of heart, the adamant of mind, who refuse to move, to grow, to accept the inevitable.

Everyone must change interiorly, advancing in love and service. Perfection lies in loving You, Lord. Sinners become Saints. Love is only love if it is selfless. We deny our very selves for Your honor and glory. Help us to continually change for the better. I love You, Lord.

———————

I AM afraid that as the serpent deceived Eve . . . your thoughts may be corrupted from a true commitment to Christ.
— 2 Cor 11:3

Be on Guard

St. Paul in his second letter to the people of Corinth tells them of his love. He also warns them. Lord, Paul is like our parents. Parents love their children. They caution them thousands of times, reminding them of dangers.

Those engaged in the sport of fencing call out "En garde" ("Be on guard") at the point of attack. Believers must be sober and alert. They candidly admit weakness, and seek their strength from You. Lord. We can always depend on Your grace. I love You, Lord.

DO not let evil talk pass your lips; say only the good things people need to hear.
— Eph 4:29

APR.
22

Tailoring Our Speech

"If you can't say something good about someone, don't say anything bad." Lord, this is an old expression seldom heard anymore. There was such a thing as being uncharitable in speech. It was listed in the examination of conscience.

Vulgarities and profanities are slow to surface from persons who always make it a point to communicate honestly and kindly. This is easy to observe when we are mindful that You love the people we address. I love You, Lord.

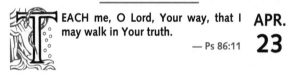

TEACH me, O Lord, Your way, that I may walk in Your truth.
— Ps 86:11

APR.
23

More Precious Than Gold or Silver

Lord, in the *Liturgy of the Hours*, recited by bishops, priests, deacons, and even lay people, there is a striking antiphon: "More precious than gold or silver is the way of life You teach us." Your way of life brings greater dividends. And we are talking eternity here.

You have sent Your Son and He has clarified our relationship. If we are loving, we succeed. The fullness of Your love, Lord, is found in Your Son, Jesus. We have His word and example. His crucifixion certifies Your love for eternity. I love You, Lord.

YOU shall love the Lord your God with your whole heart, and with your whole soul, and with all your strength.
— Deut 6:5

Capsulizing the Message

Lord, the human mind works swiftly. Hear a jingle, hum a tune, and purchase a drink. Slogans capsulize messages, and sell products. Selective words communicate.

A prayerful antiphon declares: "If anyone takes to heart what Christ has said, he will know perfect love." Now why isn't this line popular, a household phrase? "What must I do to gain eternal life?" asked the rich young man (Mt 19:16). Referring to the Mosaic Law, Jesus confirmed that it was loving You with our whole heart and soul. I love You, Lord.

NO treasure like a healthy body; no happiness like a joyful heart.
— Sir 30:16

Joyful Love

We do well, Lord, to follow the Saints who reflect the image of Christ. Among the many, St. Francis of Assisi is a person appreciated for his simple and sincere life. Those who are Christians follow Christ. Francis walked in Jesus' footsteps. His was a joyful love.

Saints are not sad people. Exteriorly they live lives like everyone else. Interiorly they are in communion with You, Lord. There is a contentment in being loved by their God. Joy fills their hearts. I love You, Lord.

HE just man rejoices in the Lord and seeks refuge in Him.

— Ps 64:11

Rejoicing in God's Love

Knowing that we are loved is a reason to be glad. Lord, there are people who seldom reflect on this simple and evident truth. You love each and every person with a tremendous love. There is grace and security in Your love.

This is a foretaste of what is to come. There will be a happiness that will last forever. How do we know that You love us? So many ways, but especially because You sent Your Son. A few minutes of meditation each day flavors our soul. I love You, Lord.

 HOUT with joy to the Lord, all the earth; sing songs to Him, sing praise.

— Ps 98:4

Sing for Joy

Sometimes we break into song. Happiness bursts forth from the heart. Lord, it is good to see happy people. Praying to You should make all of us optimists. Song springs spontaneously when we experience Your love for us.

Nothing less than a realization of Your love can fill us with such joy. When Your grace touches our souls, we want to dance in the streets. Inspire us with a true spirit of celebration. Let the hymns and antiphons resound with gladness, with music that delights the heart. I love You, Lord.

SK, and it shall be given you; seek, and you shall find; knock, and it shall be opened to you. — Mt 7:7

God Answers

"The Lord answered me when I called in my affliction" (Ps 120:1). Lord, how sad it is when people say, "If God answers my prayers." Jesus tells us to ask and we will receive. He illustrates the truth that You care for us as a loving Father.

There is no prayer that is not heard. Your comprehension is limitless. Your will is flawless. Of course, You respond with greater gifts. Your love is beyond measure. We have only to focus on Your wisdom and generosity. There is no question of Your love. I love You, Lord.

EEK no revenge and bear no grudge against your fellow countrymen.
— Lev 19:18

Grudges

No one should have a grudge against You, Lord. You do nothing wrong and everything right. Whatever Your decisions, they are rendered lovingly. Sad to say there are men and women who are bitter and blame You for their crosses.

If we wish to be at peace, we must rid ourselves of ill feeling. All wrongs must be endured patiently. Returning good for evil has a way of winning even hardened hearts. There is no other path than to love. Your way! I love You, Lord.

THE Lord, your God, is testing you to see if you really love Him with all your heart. — Deut 13:4

Testing! Testing!

Those who prepare sound systems often say "Testing! Testing!" Are their voices coming through? And Lord, is Your voice coming through?

You have created us to exercise freedom, individual judgment and decision. But Jesus teaches us to say, "Thy will be done!" There is no contradiction. We are free to choose and our choice should always be Your holy will. Our lifetime relationship is built upon love. Is there a more delightful challenge? I love You, Lord.

———————

A CHEERFUL glance brings joy to the heart. — Prov 15:30

Cheerful

Lord, another way to show love is by being polite and courteous. Respect and esteem for each and every person on the face of the earth is in order for those who love You. What other way is there for us to treat people than to embody Your care and compassion?

All who follow Christ are invited to maintain a public relationship from the heart. Our cheerfulness has positive results. Our cheerfulness says something about our own trust and confidence in You. I love You, Lord.

THE Lord's love for us is strong; He is faithful forever. Alleluia.

— Ps 117:2

MAY 2

Alleluia

Many people use the word "alleluia." It is a joyful shout. Not everyone knows that "alleluia" means "praise the Lord." For some the word springs forth spontaneously when things go right, the goal is reached. Others truly intend to glorify You, Lord.

Saints seem to focus on You, Lord. Their sights are beyond the here and the now. Their hearts and minds are lifted. They experience their Creator above His creations. Love is the reason and cause of their prayer. I love You, Lord.

I WILL teach the wicked Your ways, and sinners shall return to You.

— Ps 51:15

MAY 3

Assisting in Salvation

Lord, You invite us to assist Your plan of salvation. If we help sinners change the direction of their lives, we cooperate with Your grace. Jesus came to call those who have strayed.

St. Peter says, "If anyone speaks, let it be with the words of God; if anyone ministers let it be with the power of God" (1 Pet 4:11). This is a blessed and wonderful calling. How privileged and rewarding to be instruments of grace. I love You, Lord.

YOU shall love the Lord your God. You shall love your neighbor. On these two commandments depends the whole Law. — Mt 22:37-40

The Whole Law Summed Up

St. Paul said the whole Law is summed up in love. He was speaking of the many legalities of the Mosaic Law, which seemed to cover almost every facet of living. While laws are given to preserve order, many people felt overgoverned. Jesus presented a new, fresh approach.

Christ said, "Take My yoke upon you and learn from Me, for I am meek and humble of heart; and you will find rest for your souls" (Mt 11:29). He came not to abolish the Law, but to bring it to perfection. The relationship between heaven and earth is characterized by love. I love You, Lord.

I KNOW that the Lord is great. He is greater than all gods. — Ps 135:5

How Great Is Our God!

Scenic vistas are breathtaking. Mountains reflect Your majesty, Lord. The panorama of color in fall foliage, forest streams cascading in rainbows, and the rhythmic roar of ocean waves all inspire us to sing, "How great is our God!"

If there is delight in experiencing Your handiwork in nature, how much more is in store for us in the next life! One day we will bask in Your loving presence. Our challenge is to fulfill Your holy will in our personal lives. Let nothing overshadow our efforts. I love You, Lord.

EAR not, for I have redeemed you, and called you by your name.

— Isa 43:1

Redeemable

We have to believe that people are more redeemable than coupons, Lord. Otherwise Jesus would not have come to our world. Folks do value their coupons. Let's hope they cherish more the price Jesus paid for our sins.

And despite hardened hearts, everyone is lovable, capable of reform. There are no hopeless cases for You, Lord. Dismas was a man who repented hanging on his cross next to Jesus. Judgment is Yours, not ours. Increase our love so that it may embrace everyone. I love You, Lord.

OUR Father in heaven . . . makes His sun rise on the good and the evil, and sends rain on the just and the unjust.

— Mt 5:45

No One Unlovable

Lord, holiness takes form and shape in Saints who demonstrate heroic virtue. Love must grow to reach our neighbor. No neighbors are excluded—not even those who seem unrepentant! Jesus tells us to love our enemies, to do good to those who hate us.

In His agony, while shedding the last drop of His Precious Blood on the Cross, Jesus prayed, "Father, forgive them for they do not know what they are doing" (Lk 23:34). Christians hear Christ's voice: "Come, follow Me!" Sustain us with Your grace. I love You, Lord.

J UST as the body without the spirit is dead, so faith also without works is dead.

— Jas 2:26

True Love

Love takes substance in genuine works, Lord. It is demonstrated by acts of kindness and unselfish deeds. Wishful thinking is only a flight of fancy. All the love songs ever composed can echo through the heavens, but they must be endorsed in some way.

And You, heavenly Father, know the sincere of heart. Dedicated men and women sacrifice and suffer for those they love. There are crucifixes hanging in homes inspiring members with the ultimate sacrifice of Your Son. I love You, Lord.

HEREFORE, a man shall leave father and mother, and shall cleave to his wife; and they shall be two in one flesh. — Gen 2:24

Hand in Hand with God

"It is not good for man to be alone." These are Your words, Lord, in the Book of Genesis (2:18). Adam was not destined to live on earth without a companion. And so You created Eve and instituted marriage.

You join husbands and wives, Lord. This is part of Your Divine Plan. Their wedding vows dedicate them to one another and to You. Joined in matrimony they are surely meant to be hand in hand with You. I love You, Lord.

ERE we have no lasting city, but we seek the one that is to come.

— Heb 13:14

Properly Oriented

Jesus would not have taught us to love You, Lord, with our whole heart and soul, if our lives would be off target. Our priorities are correct when they are centered in You. Only You can satisfy our hearts. How empty life is without You!

You do not command us without reason. The greatest of commandments is to love You. The commandments are an expression of Your will. They direct us to You. Following them, we are properly oriented. I love You, Lord.

E imitators of God as very dear children and walk in love as Christ also loved us.

— Eph 5:1-2

Priceless Love

Technology improves with time. And research costs money. So the price of communication rises. Happily, our communication with You, Lord, never goes up in price. Radio, television, film, and press, all are gifts that, if rightly used, unite us with one another on earth.

Prayer unites us with You in heaven. You teach us to speak the language of love. Our plea is for everyone to rejoice in their good fortune and to assist those less fortunate. Love embraces everyone. I love You, Lord.

AM held by vows that I have made to You, O God. I will offer You a sacrifice of praise. — Ps 56:13

Baptismal Vows

True Christians have a commitment to Jesus Christ. This does not mean occasional prayer and optional worship. Lord, many of those baptized in infancy are surprised to know that they have baptismal vows.

Adult converts, those who choose to become members of Your Church, are very much aware of their vows. As seriously as brides and grooms pledge their love and fidelity at the altar, so do we commit ourselves to a loving relationship with You. I love You, Lord.

 Y heart says, "Seek His face." Your face, Lord, do I seek. — Ps 27:8

Eternal Longing

Is there any legitimate reason for wanting to die? No one should attempt to usurp Your dominion over life and death, Lord. Some may be so stressed that they think about dying to escape. That is never a good idea.

Nevertheless there are Saints who long to be united with You, Lord. Their love has reached a stage where they look forward to a face to face encounter. It is remarkable that men and women arrive at this ideal state. This eludes most of us. I love You, Lord.

OUR love is better than life; my lips shall declare Your praises.

— Ps 63:4

Open My Lips

Every morning throughout the world bishops, priests, religious, and laity start their day saying, "Lord, open my lips, and my mouth will proclaim Your praise." They chant psalms and sing hymns. They pray their Breviaries (their prayer books) in silence and in community.

Our very prayerful thoughts are inspired by You, Lord. Your holy word recorded in the Bible forms the basis of our thoughts and desires. Love is written on each page. Love is the bridge between heaven and earth. I love You, Lord.

 OU . . . shall bring forth a Son; and you shall call His name Jesus. He shall be called Son of the Most High.

— Lk 1:31-32

The Son of God

How secure we are in Your love! Lord, You so loved the world that You sent Your Son, Jesus. We read about His earthly life. He was born in a cave. The King humbles Himself. His humility becomes overwhelming even to the sacrifice of the Cross.

Everything Jesus did, everything Jesus said, tells of His love and of Your love. We are stayed from hell and invited to heaven. The road to eternity is lined with unspeakable love. You and Your Son thought about us individually and personally. I love You, Lord.

BY charity serve one another. For the whole Law is fulfilled in one word: You shall love your neighbor as yourself.
— Gal 5:13-14

MAY 16

Service with a Smile

Jesus said He came not to be served, but to serve. If anyone wants to be great, he must strive to become the least. Lord, it is a blessing and privilege to serve. Moreover, it is Your holy will. Advice, almsgiving, helping hands, all are occasions to respond.

Every courtesy and kindness should be service with a smile. After all, we are extending love to those that You love. Christians have been baptized. They have a solemn pledge to follow Christ. I love You, Lord.

GIVE thanks to the Lord, cry out His name. . . . Sing praise . . . proclaim His marvelous deeds! — Ps 105:1-2

MAY 17

Singing Praises

Whistling while we work, and humming merry tunes, tells people there is a song in our hearts. The Psalmist says something about our relationship with You, Lord. "I will sing to the Lord all my days. I will sing to God while I live" (Ps 104:33).

Religion is not merely reciting prayers and vocalizing hymns. It is a personal relationship that gives expression to the heart. There is no reason not to be happy when we count our blessings. I love You, Lord.

YOU will be hated by all for My name's sake; but he who endures to the end will be saved.

— Mk 13:13

Endurance

St. Gregory encourages us to endure all things, even to thank You, Lord, for what befalls us. "If only we could be what we hope to be, by the great kindness of our generous God! He asks so little and gives so much."

Challenges, thankfully received, can serve to win salvation. There is mystery in suffering. Perhaps it is necessary purging. A diamond does not sparkle unless it is cut. Jesus experienced agony. We look to the crucifix for inspiration and strength. I love You, Lord.

WE were buried with Him by baptism into death . . . that we also may walk in newness of life.

— Rom 6:4

New Person

After a hard, hot day working, a plunge in the pool or a few minutes under the shower makes one feel like a new person. That is the way we ought to feel after Baptism. This Sacrament makes us one with Christ. So to speak, we are "born again."

St. Paul said, "Strip off the old self with its past deeds and put on a new self" (Col 3:9-10). Christ's followers reverse their direction. No more anger. Malice, insults, and foul language are out. We change willingly, and change is refreshing. I love You, Lord.

WHATEVER you ask in My name I will do, in order that the Father may be glorified in the Son.

— Jn 14:13

MAY 20

Immediacy

There is no delayed action in our loving relationship. Lord, there is an immediacy in our prayers. You hear us as soon as the thoughts and words are formed. There is no fear of faulty transmission. This may happen in technology. It does not occur with faith.

There are some people who say "*If* God hears me." Our trust must be beyond that. A child leaps into his father's arms. Hesitation does not enter his mind. Love is very reassuring. I love You, Lord.

CRY out to the Lord: "You are my Lord, You are my only good."

— Ps 16:2

MAY 21

In Love

Some people may question, Lord, whether it is possible to fall in love with You as they fall in love with sweethearts. The Song of Songs, the Old Testament classic, describes a lover singing the praises of his beloved. His heart leaps like a stag, so joyful is his spirit.

Since You are the origin of everything good, the goodness we see in others was first in You. We may begin to understand how the Saints related. It is as if You reached out and touched their souls. It helps to illustrate and to inspire. I love You, Lord.

IS disciples said, "Lord, teach us to pray." He answered, "When you pray, say: 'Father, hallowed be Thy name. . . .' "   —Lk 11:1-2

MAY 22

Taught to Pray

Lord, we know how to pray. Jesus taught us the "Our Father." The words and phrases provide the appropriate approach and the ideal disposition of heart.

"Hallowed be Thy name." Your name is sacred. You are God. We ask for our needs and graces in a most fitting way. This prayer is a textbook on how to relate. Other prayers (formal or spontaneous) are eloquent and expressive, too. Our loving relation with You is to be cultivated. Jesus teaches us to pray and to relate. I love You, Lord.

HE Lord reproves those He loves and chastises the son He favors.

— Prov 3:12

MAY 23

Stepping Stones

Stones strategically placed in a stream allow us to "walk on water." Well, almost, Lord. It is strange how people react to crisis and tragedy. Some look up and see the stars. Others look down into the muddy ground.

Challenge and difficulty can draw us closer to You. Setbacks and sufferings are stepping stones to something better. How pleasing it must be to observe men and women taking up their crosses and following after Jesus. I love You, Lord.

EITHER death, nor life . . . can separate us from the love of God, which is in Christ Jesus. — Rom 8:38-39

MAY 24

Unspeakable Love

Words are inadequate, Lord, when it comes to describing Your love. This is understandable. Human powers are limited. Occasionally we are speechless. Something is awesome. Perhaps it is a mountain stream cascading over a cliff.

But in the peace and quiet of meditation, when complete focus is on You alone, we realize that Your love is beyond great. Your love envelops our very being. We read the Scriptures, Your Holy Word, and the magnanimity of Your care and concern overwhelms us. I love You, Lord.

ET these things be written for a generation to come, and let a people that shall be created praise the Lord.

MAY 25

— Ps 102:19

Reason for Being

The old "penny catechism" explained succinctly, Lord, why You created humans. "God made me to know Him, to love Him, and to serve Him in this life, and to be happy with Him forever in heaven."

Yet this escapes many people. Their reason for being is not clear, their justification for existence undiscovered. Out of love You brought every person from nothingness into being. And our ultimate goal is to please You, to respond to Your love. I love You, Lord.

AVE the same attitude toward all; do not be proud but associate with the lowly.
— Rom 12:16

Name Droppers

There are those who seek to impress us, Lord, by dropping names. Politicians, sports personalities, actors, and others with notoriety, are cited. It is suggested that these associations are important.

Your love embraces everyone, regardless of station in life, wealth, or good looks. Those who are poor are not to be considered second-class citizens. Those with status and fame do not rank higher in Your sight. The Divine perspective is wider. I love You, Lord.

N all your ways remember Him, and He will guide your steps.
— Prov 3:6

Attitude toward God

Wisdom leaps from the pages of Proverbs. "Have confidence in the Lord with all your heart, and do not rely on your own intelligence" (Prov 3:5). The human mind is no match for the all-knowing God. Humility is not only in order, it is a requisite.

We please You when we pray confidently and submissively. You are our loving heavenly Father. There is no fear embracing Your holy will. Jesus tells us that unless we become like little children, we shall not enter the kingdom. I love You, Lord.

ONOR the Lord with your wealth; give Him the first of your produce.

— Prov 3:9

MAY 28

Money

Lord, in our lives, thousands of dollars will pass through our hands. Paychecks are spent on cars, and houses, and vacations, and insurance, on and on.

Since we love You, Lord, how will our stewardship reflect the love we profess? When we write our checks are You on the top of the list? On the bottom? Do church and charity have priority? Or do they share the leftovers? Undecided? Wisdom suggests planning, budgeting, designating. I love You, Lord.

 OU shall love the Lord your God with your whole heart, and with your whole soul, and with your whole mind.

—Mt 22:37

MAY 29

Loving God More

There is a grace You never refuse, Lord. To love You more always meets with Your approval. This does carry with it great challenge. We cannot say, "Thy will be done," and conclude there is nothing else to do. Reaching perfection demands practice.

Love is the driving force, the pure motivation to serve. Underlying this desire is an appreciation for You and You alone. The longer we live, the greater our understanding that this service is unconditional. No strings attached. I love You, Lord.

EEK the Lord while He may be found; call upon Him while He is near.

— Isa 55:6

MAY
30

Divine Presence

All the world is invited to acknowledge Your Divine presence, Lord. Every voice is to proclaim "This is the kingdom of God!" Sincere prayers reflect the depth of the real relationship between us.

People who fail to worship, You do not love less, because Your love is unconditional. How to awaken them? Lives are enriched, mindful of Your nearness. Of all the messages to be delivered, none is more essential than the love You have for us. I love You, Lord.

T dawn may the Lord grant faithful love that I may sing praise through the night.

— Ps 42:9

MAY
31

Everyday Prayer

Religious articles serve to remind us of our relationship with You, Lord. Statues, pictures, and crucifixes in some small way recall history—Christ's true presence in time. His journey in our world was, however, for our eternity.

Jesus' life and sacrifice declares, "I love you." It does everyone good to repeat the words. This simple prayer orients our lives. This is our vocation, our calling. We advance in holiness by renewing our love morning, noon, and night. I love You, Lord.

RAY without ceasing. In all things give thanks; for this is the will of God in Christ Jesus for all. — 1 Thes 5:17-18

JUNE
1

Let Nothing Deter

We do not always feel like praying, Lord. Perhaps our minds swim and exhaustion saps our spirit. Even the Saints told about times of great dryness in their prayer life. This does not mean that You have abandoned us.

When Christ hung on His Cross, He cried out: "My God, My God! Why have You abandoned Me?" (Mt 27:46). His sufferings were intense. And of course, You did not abandon Your Son. In calm and in storm You are not far away. I love You, Lord.

 HE Lord will give strength to His people; the Lord will bless His people with peace. — Ps 29:11

JUNE
2

Strengthening Our Resolve

When Jesus felt the pressure growing, He took time off to pray. When the crowds pressed Him for healings and cures, Christ edged Himself into the desert or on a mountaintop. There He got in touch, heavenly Father.

Resolve has to be renewed. That's what retreats are for! Today men and women engage in religious exercises in convents and monasteries. They listen to Your holy word in peace and quiet. Love is not just hearts and flowers. It is centered in the will. I love You, Lord.

O there remain faith, hope, and charity, these three; but the greatest of these is charity. — 1 Cor 13:13

JUNE
3

The Only Way

Saying, "I love You," is easy to do. Demonstrating love is something else. Lord, give me strength to back up these words. Let me not kneel in church with good intentions, then, return to the streets, unmindful of my firm resolve.

When things go right, we smile and return cheery greetings. However, when tired and irritable, we become unkind, and testy. All the people we encounter are loved by You. Love calls for a constant. Love is the only way. I love You, Lord.

OURS is the day and Yours is the night; You have made the moon and the sun. — Ps 74:16

JUNE
4

A Good Day

No one is displeasing to You, Lord, when they set out to be loving. To become rich and famous means nothing in comparison. Often, when we are saying good-bye to friends, they say, "Have a good day!"

What makes for "a good day"? Minimal stress and very minute crises? If there is a gauge, a scale, our waking hours are blessed when completely dedicated to loving You. At the end of our earthly life, we pray there will have been many "good days." I love You, Lord.

B E doers of the Word and not hearers only.

— Jas 1:22

Testament to God's Love

The Bible has an Old Testament and a New Testament. It is a collection of many books written before and after Christ. Down through the long centuries, You communicated, Lord. The pages tell of Your kindness and mercy in the face of man's sins.

But at a point of time You sent Your Son to redeem us. This is the ultimate gesture of love. Jesus laid down His life so that we might live for eternity. Jesus mapped the course. He defined the road to be followed. Love is Your testament. I love You, Lord.

———

A LL the paths of the Lord are mercy and truth to those who observe His covenant.

— Ps 25:10

Forgiving

"How many times am I to forgive," Peter asked, "seven times?" Jesus replied, "No! Seventy times seven!" (Mt 18:22). And that, too, is love. Mercy is an extension of love. We are blessed, Lord, in Your forgiveness.

And if we are loving, we forgive those who trespass against us. St. Paul says, "Love is not joyful over wrongdoing, but rejoices with the truth" (1 Cor 13:5-6). The great commandment tells us that we must love our neighbor as ourselves. We rejoice in Your truth. I love You, Lord.

ROM the greatness and the beauty of created things their Creator is seen.

— Wis 13:5

JUNE 7

Knowing and Loving

"God made me to know Him, to love Him, and to serve Him. . . . " Famous catechism words! Lord, some people may ask how they can love someone they cannot see.

Scripture says, "For all men were by nature foolish who were ignorant of God, and who from things seen did not attain to knowing Him Who is" (Wis 13:1). Lord, the commandment to love You would not have been given if knowing You and loving You were not possible by dwelling on Your works in the material and supernatural order. I love You, Lord.

 EING rich, He became poor for your sakes, that by His poverty you might become rich.

— 2 Cor 8:9

JUNE 8

The Loving Poor

Do the poor have an advantage when it comes to loving You, Lord? The Beatitudes read, "Blessed are the poor in spirit. . . . " Jesus chose to be born in poverty. Mary gave birth in a tiny cave used to house animals.

Saints have vowed themselves to poverty, as if freeing themselves from burden. Those who have very few of the goods of this life often excel in appreciation of little things. They appear to be more content than the rich. I love You, Lord.

BE filled with the Spirit . . . giving thanks always . . . in the name of our Lord Jesus Christ to God the Father.

JUNE 9

— Eph 5:18-20

Thanksgiving

Lord, our days should resonate with thanks. Gratitude flows from an appreciative heart. What is there in existence that we have not received? Appreciation brings peace to the soul. St. Paul advises everyone to pray with thanks, always.

Lord, creation in all its forms and shapes, categories and colors, springs from Your love. "Oh, what a beautiful morning . . ." is a song fitting at every sunrise. In good times and in times of challenge, You are to be praised. Since You are love itself, only love comes forth. I love You, Lord.

FOR God commands the Angels to watch over you in all your ways.

JUNE 10

— Ps 91:11

Angels

Angels are persons with minds and wills. They are intelligent spirits who do Your bidding, Lord. Messengers of grace! Angels have a part in the history of our salvation. The Bible mentions them many times.

Guardian Angels are often shown in pictures watching over children. We do well to respect these unseen guardians. Directed by Your love, Angels guide us to good and away from evil. There are so many ways that Your love enhances our lives. I love You, Lord.

ER sins, many as they are, shall be forgiven her, because she has loved much.

JUNE 11

— Lk 7:47

Covering Offenses

St. Peter, quoting the Book of Proverbs, says, "Charity covers a multitude of sins" (1 Pet 4:8). This sounds logical, Lord. Sin rejects Your love and Your counsel. "I'll do it my way!" But if someone repents, turns their life around, they win Your favor.

"Hatred stirs up strifes, but love covers offenses" (Prov 10:12). History abounds with stories of conversion. Sincere people become enlightened and change their ways. They discover there is really no way to live except Your way. I love You, Lord.

HO shall ascend the mountain of the Lord? The innocent of hands and the pure of heart.

JUNE 12

— Ps 24:3-4

Climbing the Mountain

Many churches are built on hills or mountains. It seems to have been the custom. Lord, heaven is perceived up. Hell is perceived down in the nether regions. Heaven is both a place and a state of being.

It takes effort and motivation to rise to Your expectations. Unless Your grace lifts us, You are out of reach. In sports they talk about "elevating our game." Simply, this means loving You with our whole heart and soul. I love You, Lord.

FROM the fig tree learn this parable. When its branch is tender, and leaves break forth, you know summer is near.

JUNE 13

— Mt 24:32

Signs of the Times

"Red at night! Sailors delight! Red in the morning! Sailors take warning!" Lord, this is an old expression extending back to Jesus. He said to the Pharisees, "You know how to read the face of the sky, but you cannot read the signs of the times" (Mt 16:4).

There are obstacles to belief, roadblocks to understanding. Grasping truth is not merely intellectual. If truth is to be embraced, the will is involved. Dispositions cannot be dismissed. You bless the sincere of heart. I love You, Lord.

GOD, rich in mercy, loved us even when we were dead in our sins and brought us to life with Christ.

JUNE 14

— Eph 2:4-5

Life Again

A serious sin is called mortal. "Mors" means death in Latin. Lord, there is no greater tragedy than offending You seriously, knowingly, and willingly. We totter on the brink of hell. Alienating ourselves for eternity is a gamble with forever consequences.

There is peace leaving the confessional. "I absolve you . . . ," Jesus says through the priest confessor. The Sacrament of Reconciliation is a monument to Your love. Forgiveness brings us to life again. I love You, Lord.

THOSE whom I love I rebuke and chastise. Be earnest, therefore, and repent.
— Rev 3:19

The Challenge of Love

It is not always easy to love. Love is defined as the will to do good to others. It says nothing about reward or consolation. In loving You, Lord, there should be no questioning Your motives. Our love should be secure. We should not expect You to say, "Trust Me."

In ancient times You spoke to Abraham: "Take your son Isaac, whom you love, . . . and offer him up as a holocaust" (Gen 22:2). Today everyone knows You were testing Abraham's loyalty. But how bewildered Abraham must have been! I love You, Lord.

THE one sown upon good ground is he who hears the word and . . . bears fruit.
—Mt 13:23

Keeping God's Word

In the old days a handshake and a man's word were enough to clinch a deal. The contract was as good as one written. It was a matter of integrity. So, too, in our relationship with You, Lord.

Jesus said, "If anyone loves Me, he will keep My word" (Jn 14:23). Love and commitment go hand in hand. Those truly in love do not want it any other way. It is good for us to realize that You are with us, Lord, in all the twists and turns of life. I love You, Lord.

ITH You is the fountain of life, and in Your light we see light.
— Ps 36:10

You Light Up My Life

Jesus said, "I am the light of the world" (Jn 8:12). If we follow Christ, we do not walk in darkness. What makes something good? What makes something bad? What is the bottom line for conduct? Are there absolutes, or just a series of relative choices?

Lord, centuries ago, the Psalmist wrote, "Your will is wonderful indeed; therefore, I obey it" (Ps 119:129). In Your goodness, You have sent Your Son. Christ articulates Your holy will. I love You, Lord.

 O me . . . was given the grace to announce the good news and to enlighten all men as to the mystery hidden from ages past.
— Eph 3:8-9

Enlightenment

The darkening of the mind and the weakening of the will are said to be consequences of original sin. Finding answers and discovering directions presents challenge. We depend on Your inspiration, Lord.

It is always good to follow Your holy will, a course chartered in love. Nevertheless, applying it to everyday details calls for interpretation. We depend on Your grace. We call upon the Holy Spirit to clarify our thinking. Lead us, kindly Light. I love You, Lord.

HATEVER you ask for in prayer, believing, you shall receive.
— Mt 21:22

JUNE 19

No Strings

On the night before He died, Jesus thought of us. He prayed at the Last Supper. Lord, Christ inspired His disciples with confidence: "If you ask Me anything in My name, I will do it" (Jn 14:14). That's a promise with no strings.

Jesus was at the crowning moment of His loving sacrifice. He transubstantiated the bread and wine into His Body and His Blood. Hours later, on the Cross, He would offer Himself for our salvation. It was as if He declared "I cannot love you more!" I love You, Lord.

———————————

 ESUS stood in their midst and said to them, "Peace be with you! It is I, do not be afraid."
— Lk 24:36

JUNE 20

Peace

When Jesus rose from the dead, He greeted His followers: "Peace be with you!" However guilty they may have felt about scattering when He was taken captive, Christ calmed them. Lord, You provide a peace that the world cannot give.

There are times when we are worried about running off, about sinning, about whatever. Your love is our consolation. Jesus Himself experienced fear and anguish in the Garden of Olives. We are only human. Come and comfort us! I love You, Lord.

ROM the beginning I am the same, and there is none that can deliver out of My hand. — Isa 43:13

Yesterday! Today! Forever!

St. Paul watched over many families of faith. Paul the great missionary, preached to the Corinthians, Romans, Ephesians, and more. Lord, You sustained him lovingly through shipwreck, imprisonment, and torture.

The Christian faith was established in hearts by patience, perseverance, and suffering. "Jesus Christ is the same yesterday, today, and forever" (Heb 13:8). We know that the fullness of Your love is embodied in Christ, and the fullness of Christ is embodied in His Church. I love You, Lord.

OMMAND the children of Israel that . . . a lamp may burn always in the tabernacle of the testimony. — Ex 27:20-21

The Sanctuary Light

In silent respect, Lord, the sanctuary lamp glows near the tabernacle. The flame draws attention to the presence of Jesus Christ. Physically and sacramentally dwelling in the church, Christ opens His arms to embrace us. He is the Light of our lives.

Lord, You so loved all of us that You sent Your Son. Emmanuel! God is with us! The Eucharist is the most intimate, most perfect form of communion between heaven and earth. What a great privilege and blessing to visit Christ in church! I love You, Lord.

IF you return and be quiet, you shall be saved; in silence and in hope shall your strength be. — Isa 30:15

Silence

Quiet times are conducive for prayer. Silence is golden. Jesus often sought solitude in the desert and in the mountains. He communicated with You, Lord. He was renewed in mind and heart.

Retreats are helpful. They let us get away from it all. We do well to free ourselves and focus directly on You. There is comfort in the tranquillity of Your loving presence. Our spiritual side is in touch. Contact and rapport help us to get to know You. I love You, Lord.

ALL his kindred, and all his generation continued in good life, and in holy conversation. — Tob 14:17

Conversation

Some people say they talk to You all day long, Lord. There is a running conversation. This must be pleasing as long as the exchange is not limited to "gimmies," give me this, give me that.

The Psalmist prays well: "In the morning let me know Your love for I put my trust in You. Make me know the way I should walk" (Ps 143:8). The conversation is alive with the dynamics of daily details. We rejoice with our blessings. We ask for enlightenment so that Your will is accomplished. We praise You for Your generosity. I love You, Lord.

ALL will know that you are My disciples, if you love one another.

— Jn 13:35

Same Love

John, the Apostle, was close to Jesus. There was a deep friendship, Lord, between them. John says, "If God has so loved us, we ought to have the same love for one another" (1 Jn 4:11). The next time we feel angry, and inclined to retaliate, it will be wise to pause.

You love the person bugging us. You have to show much patience with us because we all are sinners. Is it possible to love everyone, even nasty people? You would not require it if it were not possible. I love You, Lord.

IF we love one another, God abides in us and His love is perfected in us.

— 1 Jn 4:12

Bring Love to Perfection

Lord, perfection is not optional when it comes to heaven. "Be perfect even as your heavenly Father is perfect," Jesus declares (Mt 5:48). That is what it means to acquire sanctity. Only Saints pass through the "pearly gates."

Loving people is what it takes. Family members, neighbors, competitors even enemies! A tall order! This is a challenge of a lifetime. It includes kindness, and patience, and long-suffering. Christ is our Way, our Truth, and our Life. I love You, Lord.

GOD is love, and whoever abides in love, abides in God, and God in him.
— 1 Jn 4:16

God Is Love

Many people long to fall in love. It is as if it were meant to be. Song lyrics ask, "What kind of fool am I who never falls in love?" There seems to be a common goal of falling in love and living happily ever after.

But everyone should fall in love with You, Lord. "The person who is without love does not know God, for God is love" (1 Jn 4:8). A true perspective of life sees You as the source and the essence of love. It is simply elementary for those who are wise. I love You, Lord.

HE chose us to be adopted through Jesus Christ as His people, according to the purpose of His will. — Eph 1:5

Sole Purpose

St. Bernard once said, "When God loves, all He desires is to be loved in return; the sole purpose of His love is to be loved, in the knowledge that those who love Him are made happy by their love of Him."

Lord, this articulates our relationship clearly. What else can we offer You but our love? We are created for loving the source of all our blessings. When we freely choose to love You, we fulfill our destiny, and we please You. I love You, Lord.

EARN from Me, for I am meek and humble of heart; and you will find rest for your souls. — Mt 11:29

Humility

Lord, humility of soul is a pleasing disposition. Mary's *Magnificat* exalts You: "He has shown might with His arm; He has scattered the proud of mind and heart" (Lk 1:51). We do well to think kindly of others. How wise it is not to rush to judgment!

Failures and shortcomings go with human nature. "Pride goes before the fall" (Prov 16:18). How patient You are with our immaturity! As we grow in love of You, hopefully we grasp the Ultimate Reality. I love You, Lord.

LORD, our Lord, how admirable is Your name in all the earth. — Ps 8:2.

Blessing God's Name

The Psalms are a collection of 150 songs of praise. These verses, Lord, are described as "a continuous sacrifice of praise, a harvest of lips blessing [Your] name." They were written centuries ago under Divine inspiration and are part of the Church's Liturgy.

St. Augustine said, "Because God chose to praise Himself, man found the way in which to bless God." Left to our own talents we fall short. We cannot adequately phrase thoughts worthy of the limitless God. I love You, Lord.

ET the mountains shout for joy before the Lord. He comes to govern the earth with justice. — Ps 98:8-9

Peace in God's Presence

You give me peace, Lord, when I reflect on Your loving presence. And You are present everywhere. But it is not always easy to be reflective. Driving the freeways, arriving at the airport, managing unruly children, all these are occasions that stress the thought of You right out of my mind.

I long for solitude, prayerful moments, when I can enjoy Your company again. Yet I also know that I can talk to You anywhere. There is a peace that only You can provide. I see You as a loving God. I love You, Lord.

AKE heed lest you be overburdened with . . . the cares of this life, and that day come upon you suddenly. — Lk 21:34

Uneasiness

Life has a multitude of unexpected twists and turns. Without Your special grace, Lord, we may live on the edge for days. Anticipating every calamity is impossible. Inevitably there will be uncertainties and uneasiness.

How do we maintain our balance in a churning world? Fears are real, but loving You secures our confidence. St. John teaches: "There is no fear in love, but perfect love casts out fear" (1 Jn 4:18). Inspire us to perfection. I love You, Lord.

WILL close their wounds and give them health . . . and I will reveal to them the prayer of peace. — Jer 33:6

Prayer As Therapy

There are many therapies prescribed today—physical, mental, and spiritual. These are beneficial exercises to assist in restoring health. Lord, prayer is always therapeutic, but hopefully folks do not think it is merely an exercise.

Prayer is genuine communication. It is an exchange that unites mind and heart with the Source of peace. Talking with You has untold benefits. You always hear us and respond. In sickness, we confide ourselves to Your holy will. I love You, Lord.

 END [wisdom] forth from Your heavens . . . that I may know what is pleasing to You. — Wis 9:10

Resignation

Resignation, like so many other words, Lord, has more than one meaning. It can signify "giving up," relinquishing responsibilities, terminating a position. It can also mean accepting Your will peacefully.

Scripture speaks of the fear of setting sail on fragile ships: "But Your Providence, O Father, guides it, for You have furnished a pathway even in the sea" (Wis 14:3). The virtue of resignation is a great habit to enjoy. It says much about our relationship. I love You, Lord.

WILL meditate on You upon my bed; through the night watches I will think of You. — Ps 63:7

Reflection

Many people dread silence. Is conscience too loud? The sounds from radio and television are constant through the day. How different the life-style of cloistered men and women in convents and monasteries!

They spend quiet hours before the tabernacle. They meditate in the presence of Christ. Parishioners may find their way to church, too. There are times for joyful music. And there are times to be very still so that You may refresh our souls. I love You, Lord.

ET my heart rejoice in Your help; let me sing to the Lord Who has given me good things. — Ps 13:6

Giver of the Gifts

Lord, gift shops abound all over the world. Trinkets and knicknacks are exchanged. Someone remembers us. They vacation and send gifts. We send "thank you notes" and are profuse in gratitude.

If we appreciate the gift, we appreciate the giver. And everything on the face of the earth flows from Your generosity, Lord. All we see, all we touch, all we receive comes from You. Each day is a gift, ready to be unwrapped and acknowledged. I love You, Lord.

A S long as you did it for one of these least brothers of Mine, you did it for Me. — Mt 25:40

JULY 7

Service with a Smile

Waiters recount stories about attending famous personalities. Waitresses delight in telling about the movie stars and officials at their tables. Serving You, Lord, has even greater bragging rights.

Jesus said, "The Son of Man has not come to be served, but to serve" (Mt 20:28). Christ defines the relationship we should have with You as well as with one another. It is an honor to serve. Love means helping. I love You, Lord.

WISDOM delivered from sorrow those who served her. — Wis 10:9

JULY 8

No Regrets

Loving You, Lord, accomplishes everything. Jesus emphasizes that the great commandment calls for loving You with our whole heart and soul. This requires total effort.

"Love means never having to say you are sorry"—a line from a movie script! Well, we should hope so—that is, if we never offend You, never sin. Christ instituted the Sacrament of Reconciliation to extend His mercy and grant us second chances. We will never regret loving You. I love You, Lord.

LOVERS of Your Law have much peace, nor is it a stumbling block for them.
— Ps 119:165

Peace

Lord, many people talk about peace. But peace is elusive. It slips away from individuals and nations. "If you want peace, work for justice!" This slogan implies that peace is not wishful thinking. It must be actively pursued.

Lord, there are people who live in luxury while others suffer in squalor. Some seem indifferent to the plight of their less fortunate brothers and sisters. This is not according to Your plan. Whatever You command makes for a better world. I love You, Lord.

GOD created man to His own image; to the image of God He created him.
— Gen 1:27

Creativity

We share in Your creativity, Lord. You have blessed us with lively imaginations. Some people seem to be gifted. Yet all creativity derives from You.

"Name something that you have not received," St. Paul challenges. "If, then, you have received it, why are you boasting as if it were your own?" (1 Cor 4:7). Grant that every stroke of the artist's brush, and every chip from the sculptor's chisel, render You honor and glory. Writers, too! I love You, Lord.

CAME that they may have life, and have it more abundantly.

— Jn 10:10

Origin and Destiny

The person who knows You, Lord, is mindful of his origin and destiny. Life is not a mystery. There is a purpose to it. World history records occasions when people did not know how to relate to You or come to You.

But You have sent Your Son, Jesus Christ. "I am the Way, and the Truth, and the Life," Christ declared. "No one comes to the Father but through Me" (Jn 14:6). And what a great destiny we have! Because of Your love, we are to live with You for eternity. I love You, Lord.

HEY received the word with eagerness, searching the Scriptures to see whether these things were so.

— Act 17:11

Searching For Gold

Lord, some people search for gold. They prospect. They dig deep within the bowels of the earth. Sad to say, there are those who become consumed in fever to strike it rich. However, Your Word says, "It is better to acquire wisdom than gold" (Prov 16:16). Values are important if they are valid for eternity.

Jesus said, "Where your treasure is, there also your heart will be" (Mt 6:21). Only love satisfies human longing. Only loving You, Lord, with our whole heart and soul brings our lives to fulfillment. I love You, Lord.

E who condones the wicked and he who condemns the just are abominable before God. — Prov 17:15

Looking the Other Way

Lord, there are times when we are encouraged to look the other way. There may be occasions when minor infractions only deserve a severe stare—for example, when a child gets caught with his hand in the cookie jar! Yet correction by parents, teachers, and superiors is also needed.

Correction is a blessing. It saves us from making the same mistakes again. Those who honestly are trying to please You, Lord, do not mind changing direction. They welcome the guidance. I love You, Lord.

HE impatient man makes a fool of himself, but the prudent one is at peace. — Prov 14:17

Anger

What is said in anger is often regretted. Lord, how patient You are with all of us! We treat one another harshly, and You see the misconduct coming. Foul words, vulgarities, vituperations, all are unnecessary when we address those that You love.

Jesus reminds us not to let the sun go down on our anger. Don't go to bed peeved. Otherwise, the night will be sleepless. And we will have something to confess. I love You, Lord.

UT I say to you, love your enemies; do good to those who hate you.

— Mt 5:44

Inclusive Love

Jesus must have startled His listeners when He declared that they were to love their enemies. Lord, Your Son taught that if we love those who love us it is no big deal. Even non-religious people do that.

St. John is emphatic. "How can he who does not love his brother, whom he sees, love God, Whom he does not see?" (1 Jn 4:20). This is the manner in which You love, Lord. Your arms encircle the globe. Everyone's potential is recognized. Christ came for the salvation of everyone. I love You, Lord.

 APPY the people who know You, Lord, who walk in the light of Your countenance.

— Ps 89:16

Ways to Happiness

Lord, what can we do to bring a smile to someone's face? If we smile at an infant, the smile comes back to us. It happens with grown-ups, too. Seeking ways to please others has its own rewards.

Cheerful folks are close to Your heart. This means that we have to develop a positive approach to people and to life. It is simply to walk in Your ways, and speak Your words, and to reflect Your sentiments. I love You, Lord.

WILL hear what the Lord God says: truly He speaks of peace to His people.

— Ps 85:9

Love and Peace

They say that love and marriage go together. Surely, Lord, love and peace go together also. There is nothing like unconditional love to calm the troubled soul.

Quiet, prayerful moments stabilize us. They put us in touch, Lord. "But You have put more joy in my heart than they have when grain and wine abound. In peace I shall lie down and sleep, for You alone, Lord, keep me safe" (Ps 4:8-9). We cannot live peacefully without You. I love You, Lord.

 S Moses lifted up the serpent in the desert, so must the Son of Man be lifted up that those who believe in Him may have eternal life.— Jn 3:14-15

The Ultimate

When Jesus was condemned to death, He did not stop loving. Lord, the world has not known a darker day. Jesus was about to come to His finest hour, His crucifixion. Christ's entire life was the ultimate sacrifice for the salvation of every soul.

There is no greater symbol of love than the crucifix. We kiss it in reverence. Lord, each time our eyes meet Jesus hanging in torture between heaven and earth, we are reminded of Your unconditional love. I love You, Lord.

GOD has set forth us Apostles . . . as men doomed to death, seeing that we have been made a spectacle to the world. — 1 Cor 4:9

A Spectacle

History relates barbaric spectacles. Lord, there have been rulers who attempted to instill fear into the hearts of their subjects. Criminals were hung in the town square. Christians were thrown to the wild beasts in the Coliseum.

And Jesus was made to bear His Cross. There was never a hesitation in His love. "Father, forgive them for they do not know what they are doing!" (Lk 23:34). His suffering expiated our sins. I love You, Lord.

SO He is the King of the Jews! Let Him come down now from the Cross, and we will believe in Him. — Mt 27:42

Aggravated Assault

Lord, today in Jerusalem Christians carry a wooden cross along the same route Christ followed. This is called *Via Dolorosa*, The Sorrowful Way. There are prayers and pauses, mindful of that dreadful day.

On the original Good Friday, there were insults. When He fell, they whipped and prodded Him to resume His death march. All this was aggravated by taunts and jeers. Not once did Jesus lash out and condemn them. This is love beyond description. I love You, Lord.

OME, all you who pass by and see if there is any sorrow like my sorrow.
— Lam 1:12

Mary's Love

Sin brought pain, suffering, and death to our world. There is no other way to explain it. Lord, we sinned, but You sent Your Son, Who is sinless, to redeem us.

As Christ carried His Cross He met His sorrowful Mother. She saw Him covered with blood, dirt, and spittle. We can only imagine her anguish. Mary's heart was fused with the will of God. She concurred with her Son's sacrifice. Her love was, like Jesus' love, a total giving. I love You, Lord.

OR neither can anyone free himself, nor render to God the price of his redemption.
— Ps 49:8

Love Pays the Price

During Jesus' death march, climbing the hill of Calvary, His tormentors feared His collapse. Lord, how much can the human body endure? The Roman soldiers compelled a man named Simon to assist the exhausted Christ. Simon shared the weight of His Cross.

Each step intensified Christ's agony. He, Who was mercy itself, would receive no mercy. All the details of Jesus' crucifixion tell of His tremendous love. This was a complete sacrifice, mentally and emotionally. Love paid the price of our sins. I love You, Lord.

B E all of one mind, compassionate, loving toward one another, merciful, and humble. — 1 Pet 3:8

JULY 23

Love and Compassion

St. James says, "Faith too, unless it has works, is dead" (Jas 2:17). Faith must be resolved into action. Lord, in every age, there are spectators and there are participants.

Tradition tells us that a woman named Veronica stepped forward despite the Roman guard. She wiped Christ's face with a towel. Legend has it that an image of Jesus's countenance was impressed on the cloth. Veronica's compassion is remembered through the years. I love You, Lord.

F OR neither does the Father judge any man, but all judgment He has given to the Son. — Jn 5:22

JULY 24

Dire Prediction

Lord, a large crowd followed Jesus as He carried His Cross. There were women whose cries filled the air. "Daughters of Jerusalem," Jesus addressed them, "do not weep for Me; but weep for yourselves and for your children" (Lk 23:28).

He predicted darker clouds on the horizon. There will be a time of reckoning. Sin offends You, Lord. While Christ offered Himself lovingly to expiate our sins, some seem to brush this aside as insignificant. Love deserves recognition. I love You, Lord.

ALLING into an agony He prayed more earnestly. And His sweat became as drops of blood falling to the ground.

— Lk 22:43-44

Psychological Pressure

Has there ever been an agony so intense as Christ's? Lord, in the Garden of Olives, Jesus perspired blood. He foresaw His torture and execution. He prayed for strength. Even His friends would flee in fear.

The psychological pressure exceeded human endurance. Christ knew what awaited Him on the summit of Calvary. But the Son of God proclaimed His unconditional love. How soul-stirring are our meditations on His Passion! I love You, Lord.

 VEN as Jonah was a sign to the Ninevites, so will the Son of Man be to this generation. — Lk 11:30

The Sign of the Cross

"No one has greater love than this, that one lays down his life for his friends" (Jn 15:13). Lord, there is nothing more to give than one's very life. Let the sight of the crucifix renew our hearts. Christ shed the last drop of His Precious Blood for us.

Christians kiss the crucifix in reverence. They hang it prominently in their homes. Respectfully, they trace the sign of His Cross on themselves. The wood and metal of this religious symbol proclaim that there is no greater love. I love You, Lord.

WHEN this mortal body puts on immortality, then shall come to pass what is written, "Death is swallowed up in victory."— 1 Cor 15:54

Triumph

Easter is a glorious day. Jesus returned to life. His Resurrection triumphs over sin and death. The world's greatest love story does not end at the tomb. Lord, Your Son died once and for all on the Cross.

He continues to offer Himself every time Mass is celebrated. Your love is written clearly on every page of the Gospels. They communicate "good news"—You love us. Christ's promise of everlasting life is confirmed. Alleluias fill the air. I love You, Lord.

NOR does anyone know the Father except the Son, and him to whom the Son chooses to reveal Him.
— Mt 11:27

Revelation

All the Books of the Bible are considered to be revelation. Lord, You drew back the curtain. People learned about You through the Prophets and holy leaders—Abraham, Moses, Isaiah, and others.

With the coming of Your Son, there was Divine intervention. God was present. All prophecies and predictions came true in Christ. Jesus is the Light of the World. We do not walk in darkness. Our relationship is defined and is characterized by love. I love You, Lord.

THE disciples asked, "What will be the sign of Your coming and of the end of the world?" — Mt 24:3

Till the End of Time

Jesus did not just come and go, Lord. After His Resurrection, Christ spent forty days reassuring His friends. He continues to guide and direct His family of faith, the Church. "Behold, I am with you always, until the end of the world" (Mt 28:20).

Today whenever a Sacrament is administrated, Christ acts. When we kneel in the confessional, Jesus absolves us through the confessor. When the priest pours the waters of Baptism, Jesus cleanses the soul. We recognize Your love. I love You, Lord.

IF you forgive men their offenses, your heavenly Father will forgive you your offenses. — Mt 6:14

No Irreconcilable Differences

In divorce courts, the phrase "irreconcilable differences" surfaces frequently. Couples declare that there is no hope of resolving conflicts.They will never kiss and make up.

In our relationship, Lord, there are no irreconcilable differences. Only harmony! You are generous, kind, and forgiving. On the Cross, our crucified Savior prayed, "Father forgive them, for they do not know what they are doing" (Lk 23:34). All Your commands are expressions of Your love. I love You, Lord.

THOSE who trust in Him shall understand truth, and those who are faithful
in love shall rest in Him. — Wis 3:9

Clear Ideas

"All the world loves a lover." So song lyrics
say. We are happy for couples who fall in
love, who discover the man or woman of their
dreams, the perfect mate. But love goes beyond mates. Unless our love embraces You,
Lord, it falls short.

All the love that we perceive in others was
first in You, the Source. Christ is quite clear
that to attain everlasting life, we must love
You with our whole heart and soul. Others are
not excluded. Because we love You, we love
others. I love You, Lord.

———

E who wishes to save his life will
lose it, but he who loses his life for
My sake will save it. — Lk 9:24

Love Empties Itself

Jesus said that no one could be His follower
unless he took up his own cross. How can this
be otherwise? Love involves sacrifice. Lord,
love is as challenging as carrying a cross.
Crosses vary, running the gamut of lifetime
trials. Christ describes the path to heaven.

How mysterious and beautiful the way to
holiness and union with You! The more love
we give, the more loving we become. How
paradoxical! The more we empty ourselves,
the more we are fulfilled. I love You, Lord.

THE Angel said to them, "Do not be afraid, for behold, I bring you good news of great joy." — Lk 2:10

Mysterious Way of Communicating

Public relations agencies seek ways to gain attention. They discern the effective ways of reaching the greatest number of people.

Lord, it appears incongruous for You to try to make Your presence felt through the obscure beginnings of Jesus. He was born in a stable. Choirs of Angels sang at Jesus' coming, although their voices did not echo around the world. Present-day technology did not exist. Yet nothing is impossible for You, Who are our loving God. I love You, Lord.

HAVE thought on my ways and turned my steps to Your decrees. — Ps 119:59

Channeling Thoughts

Politicians are adroit during interviews. Their answers reflect knowledge and skill. Command of language and intelligent phrasing are valuable talents. All of which brings us to You, Lord, and how we pray.

If talk show hosts know how to channel conversation, how much more believers should be intent in their exchange. Knowing that You look into our hearts, sincerity means more than choice of words. Direct our thoughts that we may praise and glorify. I love You, Lord.

FOR My thoughts are not your thoughts; nor are your ways My ways, says the Lord. — Isa 55:8

Do No Wrong

When we love someone we say they can do no wrong. In Your case, Lord, it is absolutely true. You make no mistakes but, we do not always give You that credit. When fate deals cruel blows, we are still in Your loving providence.

God's ways are mysterious. We cannot know all Your reasons. We do not have perspective for eternity. We cannot see down the road and around the corners. This gives us opportunity to trust Your love without questioning. I love You, Lord.

FOR this I came into the world, to bear witness to the truth. Everyone who is of the truth hears My voice. — Jn 18:37

Reality

As Jesus stood before the Roman governor, Pontius Pilate, He said that He came to bear witness to the truth. Pilate scoffed: "What is truth?" Lord, when the mind grasps reality, when the voice speaks reality, there is truth.

Christ testified to Your love. When Jesus surrendered His life in crucifixion, love for every human being was proclaimed. Christ affirmed that the goal of living was attainable only by loving You wholeheartedly. Just as He offered Himself without reservation, so will we gain eternity. I love You, Lord.

ARTHA, Martha, you are anxious about many things, yet only one thing is necessary. — Lk 10:41-42

Take the Time

Many married folks need to slow down. Lord, they work so hard. Long hours and more than one job leaves them fatigued. Some choose a simpler life. They begin to see each other more clearly and even say, "I love you" again.

All this holds for our relationship with You, Lord. How many people have said they are too busy to unite with Christ at Mass? It is necessary to take the time. This is not an "add on." It is the only way to live. I love You, Lord.

———————

F we are sons, we are heirs also; heirs of God and joint heirs with Christ. — Rom 8:17

Blending

Progress in virtue is imperceptible, Lord. It is like growth. The seed takes root, but from day to day, the eye does not discern the steady advance of the tree. Silently Your grace urges us on in loving relationship. Patience tempers our anxieties and helps us conquer adversities.

St. Paul said, "It is no longer I that live but Christ lives in me" (Gal 2:20). Christ's life and Paul's life seem to have blended. Paul's dedication and embrace of Your holy will brought about spiritual union. I love You, Lord.

ITH the proud He is stern, but to the humble He shows mercy.
— Prov 3:34

Being Humble

Jesus shows us the way. Lord, Your Son says, "Take My yoke upon you and learn from Me, for I am meek and humble of heart" (Mt 11:29). Those who are truly humble are pleasing in Your sight and attractive to everyone.

Those who are proud and haughty are difficult to deal with. In some sense, there is denial of dependency on You, Lord. An attitude of self-sufficiency! I can do it by myself. Those who excel in humility are easier to love. I love You, Lord.

ROM everyone who has been given much, much will be required; and from the one who has been entrusted with much, much will be demanded.— Lk 12:48

Accountability

The fool says in his heart there is no God. Many act as if they did not believe You exist, Lord. You have blessed us with time, talent, and treasure. Figuratively speaking, whatever we do is recorded in a big book.

Jesus told stories about stewardship. He related a parable about the master of a house returning unexpectedly. The servants who were dutiful were rewarded. Those who abused his trust were punished. Love is faithful. I love You, Lord.

THROUGH Him you are believers in God, Who raised Him up . . . so that your faith and hope might be in God.
— 1 Pet 1:21

Always Hope

Two thieves were crucified along with Jesus. One was repentant. He expressed faith in Christ. Lord, the man asked Your Son for remembrance when Jesus entered His kingdom. Grace touched his heart. There was a deathbed conversion.

Even in the most extreme and bizarre circumstances You reach out in loving mercy. You do not give up on us. Christ said to His companion in crucifixion, "This day you will be with Me in Paradise" (Lk 23:43). Where there is life, there is hope. I love You, Lord.

IF he suffers as a Christian, let him not be ashamed, but let him glorify God under this name.
— 1 Pet 4:16

Embracing God's Will

Embracing God's will is an expression of love. Lord, Jesus explained that if we love Him, we keep His commandments. Your commands in themselves declare Your love. St. Thomas Aquinas, the great theologian of the Middle Ages, pointed out that the first step toward holiness was willing it.

The quest for holiness is the same as the quest to love You unreservedly. This is true even if loving involves suffering. In the early ages, Christians were martyred. Longing for Your holy will has no strings attached. I love You, Lord.

AY the peace of God, which surpasses all understanding, guard your hearts and your minds in Christ Jesus. — Phil 4:7

AUG. 12

God's Peace

Vengeful people place obstacles in the way of their own forgiveness. Jesus called peacemakers blessed and children of God. But interior peace eludes the angry and the adamant. If they do not take to heart the need to be forgiving, bitterness sours their souls.

Well did Christ teach His disciples to pray: "Forgive us our trespasses as we forgive those who trespass against us." These are not just pious words. They are prescriptions for personal wholeness. I love You, Lord.

 OD anointed Jesus of Nazareth with the Holy Spirit and with power, and He went about doing good. — Act 10:38

AUG. 13

Power

Christ's followers learned that they were to testify worldwide. After His Resurrection, Jesus made this promise: "You shall receive power when the Holy Spirit comes upon you, and you shall be witnesses for Me . . . even to the ends of the earth" (Act 1:8).

They would proclaim Jesus Christ. The environment was hostile. Persecution and torture threatened. How would they overcome? Who would provide the energy? Nothing is impossible with You. Love conquers fear. I love You, Lord.

PON this rock I will build My Church, **AUG.**
and the gates of hell shall not prevail **14**
against it. — Mt 16:18

Defying Odds

There is no greater motivational force than
love. Lord, Christ's disciples were so motivated that they defied all odds. He commanded them to go forth and teach all nations. But all nations were not receptive.

Christians endured deprivation, torture,
and martyrdom. It was highly unlikely that
their mission would succeed. But Your love
sustained them. The family of faith grew. The
blood of martyrs is the seed of Christians. I
love You, Lord.

E who plants and he who waters are **AUG.**
equal, yet each will receive his own **15**
reward according to his labor.
— 1 Cor 3:8

Well Done

Men and women who live up to their responsibilities are rewarded. By developing
their God-given talents, they render You
honor and glory, Lord. Medals and trophies
are handed out in ceremony. This provides incentive and motivation.

But Your words, Lord are even more to be
cherished. In His parable, Jesus tells of servants who lived up to their master's expectations. "Well done, good and faithful servant!"
(Mt 25:21). There is no substitute for loving
service. I love You, Lord.

NLESS the Lord build the house, they labor in vain who build it.

— Ps 127:1

Dependency Not a Defect

We are wise to recognize our limitations. It is good to work as if everything depended on us, but pray as if everything depends on You, Lord. Everyone needs to take time out for prayer.

Jesus, too, felt the need to go apart and pray. And it is good for us to retreat, to linger in silence awaiting Your grace and inspiration. Dependency is not a defect of character. We focus on Your love and come away renewed. I love You, Lord.

HAT does it profit a man if he gains the whole world, but suffers the loss of his soul?

— Mk 8:36

Successful With God

Much is said about becoming successful in this life. Those who become wealthy are considered successful. Lord, it is true that we must work. Food, clothing, and shelter are needed. But Christ's admonition addresses ultimate success: "Seek first the kingdom of God and His justice, and all these things shall be given you besides" (Mt 6:33).

Our quest is to love You. An abundance of possessions does not make us superior. Jesus wishes us to be goal oriented. He is talking about eternity. I love You, Lord.

HEN the king will say to those on His right hand, "Come, blessed of My Father, take possession of the kingdom. . . . " — Mt 25:34

Sheep and Goats

Some time in the future, Christ will come to judge the living and the dead. Lord, this is the general judgment. How well have we loved You? Jesus said, "[The Son of Man] will separate them one from another, as a shepherd separates sheep from goats" (Mt 25:32).

Identifying with the needy, Christ says He was hungry, and thirsty, and homeless, and naked and the "sheep" came to His aid. Then He states that neglect is failure to come to the rescue of the poor and suffering. Loving our neighbors is loving You. I love You, Lord.

O faith too, unless it has works, is dead.

— Jas 2:17

Faith And Action

Faith in God, and action, go hand in hand. True belief in You, Lord, calls for loving assistance. Whoever equates love with hearts and flowers but excludes action, makes a mockery of love.

The Bible speaks of tithing. This means budgeting ten percent of income for Your purposes, Lord. What a difference our world would experience if everyone was generous! Sacrificial giving is different than sharing from our abundance. I love You, Lord.

THE person who is without love does not know God, for God is love.

— 1 Jn 4:8

AUG. 20

The Ability To Love

There is no one who cannot love. Lord, You bless everyone with this ability. To know You is to love You. Still there are those who do not show signs of knowing You, the one, true God. Millions have not encountered Your Son, Jesus.

Christ declared, "No one comes to the Father except through Me" (Jn 14:6). The human heart longs for love. Without love, there is no fulfillment. We relate through Jesus. Being lonely, deprived of love, is not in Your plans. I love You, Lord.

FOR you shall be His witness before all men of what you have seen and heard.

— Act 22:15

AUG. 21

Acknowledgments

Jesus taught His followers to acknowledge their faith. He said they were the light of the world. "Whoever acknowledges Me before others I will acknowledge before My heavenly Father" (Mt 10:32).

In Austria, people paint pictures of Jesus and the Saints on the outside of their homes. In Haiti, pickup trucks are named after Angels and Saints. Churches are silent witnesses to Your Divine Presence. Those who love You find ways to proclaim their faith. I love You, Lord.

GOD has armed me with strength and made my way secure.

— PS 18:33

My Strength

Lord, Your grace is sufficient for us. You do not permit us to be tempted beyond our capability. The Psalmist says, "O my Strength, it is to You to Whom I turn, for You, O God are my stronghold, the God Who shows me love" (Ps 59:17-18).

Our challenges are worries about business, anxieties about school, or about family members. The love that the Psalmist knew comes from the same loving God that we know. We know comfort and peace. I love You, Lord.

COME to Me, all you who labor and are burdened, and I will refresh you.

— Mt 11:28

Refreshing Pause

It is a gift to be aware of God's loving presence. There are many distractions, Lord. We can keep busy all day without giving You a thought. There is too little time to communicate. Some people even say they forget to pray.

How blessed are those who have habits of worship and prayer! One company used to promote its beverage with the slogan, "The pause that refreshes." If a soft drink can be that beneficial, how much more can moments of prayerful reflection. I love You, Lord.

APPY are we, O Israel, for what pleases God is known to us.

— Bar 4:4

Happiness

The devil, who is the Father of Lies, whispers there is happiness in sin. He tries to fake us out. Lord, there are many temptations. Underlying them all is the mistaken notion that there can be happiness without You.

You have created us for the highest blessing, Yourself. Gold, silver, power, prestige, whatever, can never satisfy the hunger in our hearts. There is peace and contentment in our conscience when we are in harmony with Your holy will. I love You, Lord.

ND they began to relate . . . how they recognized Him in the breaking of the bread.

— Lk 24:35

The Most Blessed Sacrament

Sacraments are outward signs instituted by Christ to give grace. There are seven. Of all these holy gestures one is called "The Most Blessed." This is Christ's true presence in the Eucharist.

Jesus lives in the tabernacle sacramentally. Your sanctuary is an oasis, a place of refreshment. How singularly blessed to experience Your love here on earth! You have sent Your Son. He promised to remain for all times. I love You, Lord.

UT You spare all, because they are Yours, O Lord, Who love souls.

— Wis 11:27

Think Love

Life is a merry-go-round. We repeat routines day after day, sleeping, eating, working, often under great pressure and at a frenzied pace. We race to capture fleeting hours only to find them empty, and ourselves longing for more.

Solitude sometimes proves more satisfying. Jesus demonstrated our human need to be in communication with You. That You love us is a necessary, compelling thought. We place complete trust in Your love. We are at peace. I love You, Lord.

N peace I shall lie down and sleep, for You alone, Lord, keep me safe.

— Ps 4:9

Trusting in God's Word

Many of the earlier western movies showed men shaking hands, sealing a deal. "You have my word on it," one would say. A man was as good as his word. Lord, there seems to have been more trust in those days.

Jesus once said, "Heaven and earth will pass away, but My words will not pass away" (Mt 24:35). His integrity is without challenge. His promise of eternal love is true. The declaration of His love strengthens our faith and our hope. I love You, Lord.

MYSELF will comfort you. Should you then fear mortal man?

— Isa 51:12

Comfort

There is never a time, Lord, when You are not watching over us. You are our heavenly Father and love all Your children. Jesus counsels us not to fear. You are aware of every detail, even the number of hairs on our heads.

There is comfort in knowing that You are with us. No one is tempted beyond his own strength. Gold is purified by fire. Our imperfections are purged by trial. You sustain us. We place our hand in Your hand as we walk through life. I love You, Lord.

 OUR hands made me and shaped me; give me wisdom to learn Your commands.

— Ps 119:73

Educated To Love

How blessed are those who have come to love You, Lord! This appears to be a learning process, Even though You are love itself. Parents and religious education teachers explain that we are to love You. Still these are just so many words.

Saints provide examples. We have Your revelation commanding us to love. We see how lovable people are. We experience Your love in them. Unswervingly we come to an unmistakable conclusion. I love You, Lord.

No Questions

Lord, the soul is tranquil when it accepts all Your teachings without exception. We experience interior peace when we no longer question the mysteries of faith. The mind is at rest when it smiles at every pronouncement of the Church.

Those who constantly challenge never arrive at conclusions. Life is an unending flux. Wisdom tells us to be content. We do not have a grasp on every truth. But the truths we embrace bring security. Jesus dispels doubts. I love You, Lord.

An Excellent Way

St. Paul encourages us to strive for spiritual gifts. Our destiny is eternal life with You, Lord, and this is essentially spiritual.

Paul details love as kind, and patient, and not seeking its own interest. Rudeness and jealousy are not tolerated. There is a rejoicing with the truth. To arrive at this ideal is the challenge of a lifetime. "So there remain faith, hope, and charity, these three; but the greatest of these is charity" (1 Cor 13:13). I love You, Lord.

F you ask anything of Me in My name, I will do it.

— Jn 14:14

How To Relate

Lord, it is no longer a mystery how we should relate to You. You have sent Your Son. The invisible God, the Pure Spirit, becomes visible. "The Word was made flesh and made His dwelling among us" (Jn 1:14).

Jesus declared, "He who sees Me sees also the Father" (Jn 14:9). The fullness of Your love is embodied in Jesus. The fullness of Jesus is found in His Church. And how do we please You? By embracing Your holy will as articulated by Jesus: to love You with our whole heart and soul. I love You, Lord.

UT seek the kingdom of God, and all these things shall be given you besides.

— Lk 12:31

Spending My Life

What do you want to be when you grow up? Lord, parents and friends seek to know our goals. A fireman, a policeman, a pilot, a nurse, all quite predictable answers. Some do not know what their careers will be.

But if we understand the purpose of life, loving You is paramount. No one is more deserving. Whatever profession is pursued through the years, serving You has top priority. I love You, Lord.

ESUS said, "When I am lifted up from the earth, I will draw all to Myself." He said this signifying the kind of death He was to die. — Jn 12:32-33

No Greater Love

Lord, kissing the crucifix reverently morning and evening is a loving gesture. Pondering this instrument of torture touches the depth of our souls. There can never be a greater sacrifice, one that provides universal salvation.

There are times when we become accustomed to furnishings at home and even at church. Hopefully, the sight of our Savior in His finest hour will always inspire love in our hearts. I love You, Lord.

 OW to Him Who is able to strengthen you in accordance with the Gospel, . . . through Jesus Christ, be honor forever and ever.

— Rom 16:25-26

The Power of God

Lord, You are all powerful. We call You Almighty, and this is true. "He's got the whole world in His hand," so the song lyrics say.

But St. Paul declares that the Gospel is Your power, "unto salvation to everyone who believes" (Rom 1:16). There is force, persuasion, and grace, all flowing from the good news, the Gospel. What is the good news? Christ Himself! His coming is the unique and singular communication of Your love. I love You, Lord.

I N all these things we overcome because of Him Who has loved us.

— Rom 8:37

Indomitable Love

"If God is for us, who is against us?" (Rom 8:31). Lord, St. Paul is forceful and eloquent in proclaiming Your love. He is certain that nothing can deter You from loving us.

No one has a track record like St. Paul. He was imprisoned, flogged, driven out of towns, but he pressed on. His journeys enabled him to reach countless numbers. Touched by grace, many became Christians. They, too, learned of Your love in Jesus Christ. I love You, Lord.

T HIS hope we have, as a firm and sure anchor of the soul, reaching beyond the veil.

— Heb 6:19

Fix in Your Heart

Faith must be firmly established in our hearts. Lord, Moses told the chosen people, "Know and fix in your heart that the Lord is God in the heavens above and on the earth beneath, and that there is no other" (Deut 4:39).

There has to be interior conviction. Belief is not merely intellectual. It involves the total person. There has to be an endorsement. Our entire being has to embrace You. Love does not thrive on "maybes." I love You, Lord.

B E faithful unto death, and I will give you the crown of life.

— Rev 2:10

The Crown of Life

Lord, temptation comes in many forms. True Saints meet challenges with steadfast determination. St. James tells us, "Blessed is the man who endures temptation, for when he has been tried he will receive the crown of life" (1:12).

Many people reach for things that do not satisfy the soul. Rich or poor, the heart finds peace and contentment in loving. Christ sets the standard, to love You with our entire being. Perseverance in love alone succeeds. I love You, Lord.

T O You, O my strength, will I sing, for You, O God, are my fortress, my loving God.

— Ps 59:18

Singing of God's Love

Why are not more people singing of Your love, Lord? Is there anything more impressive than Your love for us? The Psalmist says, "Blessed be the Lord Who has shown me wondrous love in a fortified city" (Ps 31:22).

Also, "I shall sing of Your strength, and extol Your love in the morning" (Ps 59:17). Attention seems to be diverted from You, Lord. It is peculiar. No one loves us more. It is unthinkable that there should be silence about Your love. I love You, Lord.

AND I will give you greater gifts than you had from the beginning.

— Ezek 36:11

Favors

Life overflows with blessings. Lord, anyone who truly knows You realizes that You are love itself. Every day is a gift. "The favors of the Lord are not consumed, His mercies are not spent. They are renewed every morning, so great is His faithfulness" (Lam 3:22-23).

How extraordinarily favored are men and women of faith! They see the world and all the experiences in Your light. They do not search for purpose for they know that You are their origin and destiny. I love You, Lord.

GOD'S love was revealed in our midst in this way: He sent His only Son . . . that we might have life through Him.

— 1 Jn 4:9

How Do You Know?

Lord, a priest, working with the First Communion class, purposely presented the children with a question and its answer. "How do you know God loves you?" The boys and girls responded dutifully in chorus, "Because He sent His Son!"

Of course, there is evidence of Your love in every aspect of creation. And when those creatures, created after Your image and likeness, sinned, You sent Jesus for their redemption. For our redemption! I love You, Lord.

LIVE in the faith of the Son of God, Who loved me and gave Himself up for me.

— Gal 2:20

Completely Christian

Lord, St. Paul was indefatigable in proclaiming Your Son, Jesus Christ. He acknowledged that he persecuted Christians before he became a Christian. His miraculous conversion is written in the Scriptures.

Paul became thoroughly involved: "I have been crucified with Christ. It is no longer I that live, but Christ lives in me" (Gal 2:19-20). This is an identification believers strive for. Paul's life is an inspiration, an encouragement to walk in Christ's footsteps. I love You, Lord.

 ANY waters cannot quench love, neither can floods sweep it away.

— SS 8:7

The Language of Love

An infant experiences love. Parents shower their baby with care and affection. Lord, this is good and admirable. Even if words are not spoken, love is communicated.

As children grow, parents cultivate their hearts by daily prayer and the formation of spiritual values. These practices, and especially participation in Christ's Eucharistic Sacrifice, enhance the children's relationship with You. They perceive Your love in the love of those around them. The language of love is universal. It is understood by all races. I love You, Lord.

UT above all these things have charity, which is the bond of perfection.

— Col 3:14

Where There Is Love

"Where there is love, there is no labor." Lord, this axiom provides insight into the hearts of so many missionaries who leave everything and follow Christ. There is no financial gain in journeys to foreign lands. They seek only to establish Your Kingdom of love.

St. Augustine preached:"The greater one's love, the easier the work" (Sermon 340). He cited Jesus' questions to Peter. "Do you love Me?" Peter affirmed his love. Christ, then, assigned the work: "Feed My lambs. Feed My sheep." I love You, Lord.

 EE that you do not despise one of these little ones; for I tell you their Angels in heaven always behold the face of My Father.

— Mt 18:10

Angels

Angels are in Your loving service, Lord. They are real persons. They have their own identity. Philosophy defines a person as an individual substance of a rational nature. Angels have minds and wills, but, as spirits, are not confined to matter.

They do Your bidding, Lord. You send them on errands of mercy. "God commands the Angels to watch over you in all your ways. In their hands they will support you, lest you dash your foot against a stone" (Ps 91:11-12). I love You, Lord.

HAS not God chosen the poor of this world to be rich in faith and heirs of the kingdom? — Jas 2:5

The Poor

Jesus said we would always have the poor with us, Lord. There have ever been the fortunate and the unfortunate. Christ identified with the poor. We read, "Turn not your face away from any of the poor, and the face of the Lord will not be turned away from you" (Tob 4:7).

We are urged to have a "preferential option for the poor." What we do for the least of our brothers and sisters, we do for You. They will know we are Christians by our love. Those with less provide opportunity for our love and generosity. I love You, Lord.

AND this is love, that we walk according to His commandments. — 2 Jn 1:6

The Call

Lord, the call to be loving often falls on deaf ears. Love means loving even if it is not reciprocated. "Seek no revenge and bear no grudge against your fellow countrymen. You shall love your neighbor as yourself" (Lev 19:18).

Bearing wrongs patiently goes with the challenge to love. Getting even is not permitted. The words of the crucified Christ echo down from His Cross. "Father, forgive them for they do not know what they are doing" (Lk 23:34). I love You, Lord.

OME, children, hearken to me; I will teach you the fear of the Lord.

— Ps 34:12

All God's Children

Lord, You have no racial prejudice. All peoples, regardless of color or ethnicity, are Your children. And You expect us to be loving. "You shall treat the stranger who resides with you no differently than the natives born among you" (Lev 19:34).

How blessed we are when we visit a foreign land and hospitality flows! We return to our homeland full of appreciation. Love is a universal language. It is understood by everyone. You have spoken and Your words are wisdom. I love You, Lord.

HAT does the Lord your God require of you, but that you fear the Lord your God, and walk in His ways?

— Deut 10:12

What Does the Lord Ask?

There are times when we stumble over the obvious. Lord, Your communication is never in need of clarification. Prophetic messages may need interpretation. But how we should relate to You is spelled out clearly.

Our lives can only be properly oriented when You are first in our thoughts. You have exclusive priority. There are to be no strange and foreign gods. You invite us to love. This is our goal and calling. Everything else is secondary. Love alone is fulfilling. I love You, Lord.

YOU will show me the path of life, the fullness of joys in Your presence.

— Ps 16:11

19

Joy

Lord, the desire for happiness is universal. You have created us with this thirst and inclination. "Fill us speedily with Your love, that all our days we may sing for joy" (Ps 90:14).

Even in ancient times, when the Psalmist was inspired to write, folks looked for peace and contentment. What blessedness we experience when we are loved. Children seek fun and excitement. They find love in a caring family. And our greatest love is found in You. I love You, Lord.

IF anyone speaks, let it be with the words of God.

— 1 Pet 4:11

SEPT.

20

Loving Words

If we really love one another, the words we speak are loving. Lord, there is not a person alive that You do not love. Jesus said that we are to love our neighbor as ourselves. And who is our neighbor? Everyone on the face of the earth.

Angry words and outbursts of temper are unacceptable. St. Paul wrote, "Do not let evil talk pass your lips; say only the good things people need to hear" (Eph 4:29). Loving words reflect our relationship with You. I love You, Lord.

LOVE the Lord Who heard my voice in supplication.
— Ps 116:1

God Listens

Lord, there are people who imagine You to be far away, distant. How can this be? You have sent Your Son, Jesus, into our world. He walked our roads and spoke personally to men, women, and children. Christ established His Church and He is with all of us until the end of time.

When we pray, there should be no doubt that You hear our prayers. There is great comfort in prayerful conversation. Even when we are in distress, You are at our side. Your love is without question. I love You, Lord.

PEN rebuke is better than hidden love.
— Prov 27:5

Kind Correction

Taking a wrong turn can lead people miles from their destination. Lord, when folks turn away from You, without question they are missing their goal in life. It is a blessing to be corrected.

Heavenly Father, Your disciplines guide us from our wayward paths. Why are we afflicted with trials? Sheep do separate from the flock. They stray. Mysteriously, You lead them back. I love You, Lord.

I WILL bring them into My holy mount, and will make them joyful in My house of prayer. — Isa 56:7

SEPT. 23

God's Guarantee

How sure are we of Your love, Lord? Your word is all the assurance anyone ever needs. "Though the mountains be moved and the hills tremble, My love shall never leave you" (Isa 54:10).

No matter what happens on earth You are with us. There are trials and challenges. Unswerving faith in a loving, caring God sustains us. Jesus declared that those who lose their lives for His sake will save their lives for eternity. I love You, Lord.

BEWARE of false prophets, who come to you in sheep's clothing, but inwardly are ravenous wolves. — Mt 7:15

SEPT. 24

Con-Artists

Lord, You chose Moses to instruct Your people. Inspired, he warned about possible pitfalls. Other prophets would come along. They might exhibit signs and wonders. These con-artists might tempt them to fall into idolatry, to worship false gods.

"Pay no heed to the words of that prophet or that dreamer; for the Lord, Your God, is testing you to learn if you really love Him" (Deut 13:4). There is a susceptibility in human nature posing danger. Temptation is a reality. I love You, Lord.

140

THOSE who seek to become rich fall into temptation and many harmful desires. — 1 Tim 6:9

Root of Evils

Money is not evil. However, Lord, the love of money turns heads and hearts. We are very susceptible to this form of temptation. St. Paul wrote: "The love of money is the root of all evils, and some people in their desire for it have strayed from the faith" (1 Tim 6:10).

How blessed are those who refuse to sacrifice their honesty out of love for You, Lord! They choose to be poor rather than offend You. They store up treasure for themselves in the next life. I love You, Lord.

LET us consider how to rouse one another to love and to good works. — Heb 10:24

Encouragement

Encouragement comes in many forms. Kind words! A pat on the back! High marks! Lord, we derive incentive from interests shown. Teammates chatter along on the baseball diamond. Cheerleaders chant in rhythm. Parents utter encouraging words.

Since love is life's ultimate goal, everyone deserves to be spurred on. If a non-lover, a sinner, can be touched by Your grace, heaven rejoices. Inspire Christians to follow their leader, Jesus Christ. May they be fired with zeal for Your holy will. I love You, Lord.

BELOVED, no new commandment am I
writing to you, but an old commandment that you had from the beginning.
— 1 Jn 2:7

From the Beginning

"Nothing is new under the sun" (Eccl 1:9).
This Old Testament saying rings true. Lord,
every discovery and invention has always
been possible. Likewise the invitation to love
is not new. "For this is the word that you have
heard from the beginning: we should love one
another" (1 Jn 3:11).

Love matures in the giving, not in the receiving. Jesus said that unless a grain of
wheat falls to the ground and dies, it remains
just a grain of wheat. I love You, Lord.

LET your manner of life be free from love
of money; be content with what you
have. — Heb 13:5

Money Worries

People have been known to take their lives
because of money worries. Great losses appear unbearable. Lord, there is relief and
freedom in loving You. Those who know You,
Lord, are convinced of Your love.

They trust. Even if their lives are threatened,
they persevere. This calls for a confidence and
a resignation, all of which is more than possible when we have a loving relationship with
You. Bless everyone with an appreciation that
brings them peace. I love You, Lord.

THE Lord looks upon those who love Him; He is their shield and support.
— Sir 34:16

Comfort and Security

A comforting picture depicts a Guardian Angel watching over children. Mothers and fathers explain the image to their sons and daughters. Lord, children come to know Your love in the Angels You assign to guard and to guide them.

We are all Your children, Lord, heirs of heaven. Christ embraces us in His Sacrament of Baptism. When our faith is alive, dynamic, and true, peace floods our souls. Jesus illustrates Your care and concern. I love You, Lord.

FOR God is not unjust, that He should forget your work and the love that you have shown in His name. — Heb 6:10

The Lord Appreciates

Nothing happens without Your knowledge, Lord. There are no secrets. While You love us unconditionally, You are delighted with loving response. When we serve one another, You consider these kind gestures as rendered to You.

Jesus says, "As long as you did it for one of these least brothers of Mine, you did it for Me" (Mt 25:40). Since Your love for each and every person is tremendous, You are pleased. It is love that unites us in heaven and on earth. I love You, Lord.

HEAVEN and earth will pass away, but My words will not pass away.

— Mt 24:35

OCT. 1

God's Word

God expresses His holy will. From the beginning of time men and women have known what is right and what is wrong. Lord, knowing Your will, and embracing it, are two different things.

St. John counsels, "In the person who keeps His word, the love of God is truly perfected. By this we know that we are in union with Him" (1 Jn 2:5). To accept Your word willingly, and to make it our own, is to embrace Your way, Christ's way. I love You, Lord.

IN my affliction I called upon the Lord . . . and from His temple He heard my voice.

— Ps 18:7

OCT. 2

Occasions of Grace

Whatever turns people in Your direction, Lord, cannot be all bad. In fact, such happenings are special occasions of grace. You are love itself, and everything You do is done lovingly. At times people ask, "Why me?"

No one wishes catastrophe on anyone. Still, bitter medicine may bring about recovery and health. Afflicted individuals may commence to thrive spiritually. How blessed are those who see Your loving hand in all life's challenges! I love You, Lord.

HOEVER does the will of God, he is My brother and sister and mother. — Mk 3:35

Love Is Dynamic

Love is a universal experience because You love everyone, Lord. Love is active, not static. It calls for action. Spiritual union with You moves us to extend Your love.

St. John says, "Children, let us love not in word or speech but in deed and truth" (1 Jn 3:18). The old adage is true: "Love tends to diffuse itself." There is a dynamic. Jesus explained that when we help the hungry, thirsty, homeless, sick, and imprisoned, it is the same as helping Him. I love You, Lord.

OW beautiful upon the mountains are the feet of him who brings glad tidings, preaching peace, bearing good news. — Isa 52:7

Communicating Love

How is love communicated? By loving! Lord, this oversimplification is on target. How does a person become loving? By willing to do good to others! Love is centered in the will. Followers of Christ are intent on communicating love.

Jesus commissioned His disciples to tell the world of the "good news" of Your love. You so loved all of us that You sent Your Son. True Christians are aware of their mandate. They are not content to wrap themselves in a cocoon. They let their light shine. I love You, Lord.

T is a sign of much kindness to punish sinners quickly rather than letting them go for long. — 2 Mac 6:13

Chastisements

Lord, for centuries misfortunes and calamities were considered corrective punishments. In Old Testament times the sacred temple was profaned by sacrilegious acts. The chosen people believed they were called to correction.

Loving parents are known to say, "This hurts me more than it hurts you." Neglect negates love. Serious challenges in life serve Divine judgment. You love those whom You chastise. Whatever happens, You care. I love You, Lord.

———————

 EHOLD, I take from you the desire of your eyes with a stroke. — Ezek 24:16

Stop Wanting It

Lord, once during a radio interview a rising star was asked what she does when she wants something and can't have it. "I stop wanting it!" she replied.

Knowing when to cease and desist, makes for wisdom. Pitting our wills against Your Divine will never will do. Peace of mind and heart comes by saying, "Thy will be done." It is advisable to thank You, Lord, in good times and in bad times. This demonstrates a trust. Thank You for Your patience. I love You, Lord.

ND Him He gave as head over all the Church, which is His body.
— Eph 1:22-23

Christ Leads

Jesus leads His followers: "I am with you always, until the end of the world" (Mt 28:20). Lord, Your Son established His Church. St. Paul eloquently explained, in the Letter to the Ephesians, that Christ is the head of the body, and Christians are members of the body.

Those who profess faith in Him are to walk His ways and speak His words. Just as the various parts of the human body work in harmony, so are all who are baptized to act as one. Christ's love is our esprit de corps. I love You, Lord.

EAR all that the Lord, our God, shall say, and then tell us, and we will listen and obey.
— Deut 5:27

The Spirit of Openness

Happy those who hear Your word in a spirit of openness, Lord. They shall bear fruit. Stubbornness closes doors. At times, we provide our own obstacles to the truth. The human heart is well disposed when eager and sensitive to Your commands.

You have sent Your Son, Jesus, as an everlasting sign of Your love. He is the Light of the World. No one walks in darkness when following Christ. How blessed are those who echo Samuel! "Speak, [Lord], for Your servant is listening!" (1 Sam 3:10). I love You, Lord.

IF, therefore, the Son makes you free, you will be free indeed. — Jn 8:36

Love and Freedom

Love and freedom go hand in hand. Lord, You are all loving and perfectly free. Without this basic freedom, people are not capable of loving. Love is an intelligent act—not instinct.

Why should we love You? Because You are infinitely lovable, You have given us life and You have given us the ability to love. When we grasp this, we enjoy a freedom and peace that the world cannot give. Jesus declared: "The truth will make you free" (Jn 8:32). I love You, Lord.

JESUS . . . , having loved His own who were in the world, loved them to the end. — Jn 13:1

The Lord Loves Me

Simple truths often elude minds. How can something be so obvious and not be seen? Lord, the story of Your love is written on the pages of history from the beginning of time. Yet it is often overlooked by us.

What a world this would be if every person meditated three minutes a day on the sentence, "God loves me!" Lives would be transformed. We view life and its realities with rose-colored glasses when we know that we are loved. I love You, Lord.

OVE, therefore, is the fulfillment of the Law.
— Rom 13:10

The Secret of Success

Lord, many people say they know the secret of success. Some who conduct seminars declare they are willing to share their secrets. However, success is equated with becoming wealthy.

But it is not a secret that the true success comes from loving You. This is the ultimate goal of life. When we appear before You on Judgment Day, love and service will tip the balance of the scale. Loving our neighbor is loving You. I love You, Lord.

HEN you pray, go into your room, and close the door, and pray to your Father in secret.
— Mt 6:6

Prayer Time

Very busy people with hectic schedules often devote time to meditation just to get a handle on life. Recollection calms the soul. Lord, the centuries' old practice of prayer is being discovered again anew.

Of course, prayer is necessary and helpful. Jesus taught His disciples to pray. Conversation builds relationships. Exchange nourishes love. Reading a Gospel meditatively is inspirational. If we run out of things to say, we can listen. I love You, Lord.

RAISE the Lord, O my soul; I will praise the Lord throughout my life. — Ps 146:2

Living To Praise

Everyone is called to praise You, Lord. You are deserving of all our praise. Our vocation is to recognize, to acknowledge, and to honor You.

Men and women in monasteries and convents chant Psalms and hymns. Praising, praying, is an integrated way of life. And so it should be for everyone in accord with their state in life. "Glory to God in the highest"—everywhere in churches and in homes. We live to praise You. I love You, Lord.

 LESSED are they who hunger and thirst for righteousness, for they shall be satisfied. — Mt 5:6

A Different Approach

Lord, Christ's prescription for happiness differs from customary expectations. Jesus preached His famous "Sermon on the Mount" with an "other world" perspective. Undoubtedly, Christ is more realistic.

Blessed are the poor in spirit, the merciful, and the meek, He advised. Peacemakers are close to Your heart. The Beatitudes have to do with ideal dispositions: how to cope under trying circumstances, how to respond to Your love. I love You, Lord.

ALLELUIA! Praise, all servants of the Lord, praise the name of the Lord.
— Ps 113:1

Alleluia!

At Easter, alleluias ring the air. This joyful word proclaims Christ's rising from the dead. Lord, many use the expression, "alleluia," but do not know that it means, "Praise the Lord!" And, of course You should be praised on the feast of the Resurrection as well as every day of the year.

How accurate we are to attribute all our blessings to You! Joy explodes from the mind and heart. With each passing day our lives become "alleluias." I love You, Lord.

THEY continued in the teaching of the Apostles and in the breaking of the bread and in the prayers. — Act 2:42

Daily Prayer

It is easier to pray when everything seems to be going well, although there may be a temptation to pray less. Lord, many turn to You in desperation, when things go badly. Is this a way to renew rapport and relationship?

There are material needs: food, clothing, and shelter. There are spiritual needs: relationships become strained at home, at work, and at school. Quiet time with You strengthens us. The human soul is lifted. We are reminded of Your love. I love You, Lord.

ET those who fear the Lord say, "His love endures forever." — Ps 118:4

Loving for Eternity

There are zillions of love songs. The lyrics tell about undying love, loving for eternity. Lord, the sentiments are understandable. People in love sing romantic things. However, the track record of lasting human relationships isn't good. Realistically, men and women fall in love, and then fall out again.

The Psalmist tells of Your love. "Give thanks to the Lord, for He is good, His love endures forever" (Ps 106:1). We do well to study Your loving ways. I love You, Lord.

E is near Who justifies me. Who will contend with me? — Isa 50:8

OCT. 18

The Nearness of God

"Have no anxiety at all . . ." (Phil 4:6). Pray, make your requests known. Lord, there is no difficulty communicating between heaven and earth. St. Paul says, "The Lord is near" (Phil 4:5). From the beginning of the world, love has united us.

Stress, unwarranted fears, and the feeling of inadequacy, all contribute to human unrest. St. Paul counsels devout, confident prayer: "May the peace of God, which surpasses all understanding, guard your hearts and minds in Christ Jesus" (Phil 4:7). I love You, Lord.

THOSE who sow in tears shall reap in joy.
— Ps 126:5

Reaping a Harvest

Anyone can begin a project. Not everyone can complete it. Lord, we humans are weak, and we become weary. It is wisdom to acknowledge that You are all powerful and that we are merely instruments of Your grace.

St. Paul declared, "Let us not grow weary of doing good, for in due time we shall reap our harvest" (Gal 6:9). He was a man with a mission to bring Jesus Christ to the world. Paul had the spirit of Christ Whose love conquers. I love You, Lord.

BLESSED be God, Who has not rejected my prayer, nor withdrawn His mercy from me.
— Ps 66:20

Accepting Answers

A child was taunted for having prayed for a wagon at Christmas. The wagon was not beneath the tree. "You prayed and God did not answer!" The little girl retorted, "Yes, He did. He said, no."

Lord, You always respond to our prayers. Jesus encourages us to ask anything in His name. But it is wisdom to understand that Your will is to be done. In the light of eternity, Your replies are appropriate and fitting. Inspire us to welcome all Your decisions because they are all Divinely inspired. I love You, Lord.

ELL done, good and faithful servant; . . . enter into the joy of your master. — Mt 25:21

Sharing Love

Love is a sharing. Boy meets girl. They fall in love and want to spend the rest of their lives together. Lord, there is joy in love. Our greatest joy is loving You, Who "are all good and deserving of all our love." We repeat this phrase so many times in reciting our Act of Contrition.

How sad it is that there are people who do not know You. We pray that all of them may be enlightened by Your grace. "What kind of fool am I who never falls in love?" the song lyric asks. And You say, "Come, share My joy!" I love You, Lord.

HIS first of His signs Jesus worked at Cana of Galilee; . . . and His disciples believed in Him. — Jn 2:11

Miracles of Love

The kindness of Christ is demonstrated in His miracles. Crowds came to Him in hope of healings. Lord, Your Son, Jesus did not disappoint anyone.

St. John tells us, "Jesus worked many other signs in the sight of His disciples that are not written in this book. But these are written that you may come to believe that Jesus is the Christ, the Son of God, and that believing you may have life in His name" (20:30-31). I love You, Lord.

E cured many of diseases, and to many who were blind He granted sight. — Lk 7:21

Sight

Two blind men cried out to Jesus, "Lord, let our eyes be opened." Lord, Your Son's heart was moved. Love and compassion welled within Him. He touched their eyes. "At once they received their sight, and followed Him" (Mt 20:33-34).

They entered a world of light. Darkness was banished. Christ, the Light of the World, beamed His grace and power. There was sight and insight. Faith filled their souls. They walked in the footsteps of the One Who blessed them. I love You, Lord.

 HICH is easier to say, "Your sins are forgiven," or to say, "Arise, and walk"? — Mt 9:5

The Paralyzed Man

Lord, friends lowered a paralyzed man through the roof. It happened in Capernaum when the crowds could not enter the home where Jesus was preaching.

"Your sins are forgiven," He said to the man on a mat. Some in the gathering thought Christ blasphemed. Despite the hostility, Jesus cured the afflicted one: "Rise, take up your mat, and go home" (Mk 2:11). And he did, much to the astonishment of all. The Gospels are about Your love to which Jesus is a witness. I love You, Lord.

IS mother said to the waiters, "Do whatever He tells you." — Jn 2:5

A Wedding

Changing water into wine was no trick. It was a miracle. Lord, when Mary explained to Jesus the predicament of the bride and groom and the many guests who came to Cana, He responded.

Mary's intercession moved her Son. They had sympathy for the man and woman who had just joined their hands and hearts in marriage. This passage witnesses Jesus' love. He continues to strengthen and affirm those vowing to love. I love You, Lord.

GIVE thanks to the Lord, for He is good; for His mercy endures forever. — Dan 3:89

Lepers

Ten lepers approached Jesus as He was traveling to Jerusalem. People shunned them and feared them, because of the danger of contagion. Lord, Christ was moved to pity. He told them to visit the priests of the Mosaic Law, who would judge their cleansing.

All ten were miraculously cured. Only one returned to give thanks. Jesus said to him, "Your faith has saved you" (Lk 17:19). Every day we can rejoice and be glad, thankful to You for the forgiveness of our sins, the cleansing of our souls. I love You, Lord.

HO, then, is this, that He commands even the winds and the waves, and they obey Him?

— Lk 8:25

Calming the Sea

Only those who have been out on stormy seas know what a terrifying experience it can be. Lord, life is like that at times.

Jesus taught His disciples a lesson. While they were on the Sea of Galilee, a squall lifted their boat and tossed it about. The disciples cried out to Jesus. He raised His arms and calmed the tempest. We find comfort, Lord, in Christ's strength. How blessed we are to know You and realize Your love! I love You, Lord.

 HEY brought Him a blind man and entreated Him to touch him.

— Mk 8:22

The Touch of a Hand

The first pope was married, as well as some others after him. St. Matthew tells us that Jesus cured Peter's mother-in-law. Lord, Your Son reached out and touched her hand. She was in bed with a fever. "She rose and began to wait on Him" (Mt 8:15).

Wherever Christ journeyed, the blind, the deaf, the lame, and the handicapped flocked to Him for healings. He reached out in love. His entire life was a labor of love. He came to bear witness to this truth. You are a God of love. I love You, Lord.

UT since you reject it and judge yourselves unworthy of eternal life, we now turn to the Gentiles. — Act 13:46

Unworthy

Lord, once a Roman centurion asked Jesus to cure his servant who was paralyzed. Christ promised to go to the man's home. The centurion said, "Lord, I am not worthy that You should come under my roof; only say the word and my servant will be healed" (Mt 8:8).

Jesus remarked that He had not found such faith in all the land. He guaranteed health, and it was given that very hour. As true God and true Man, Jesus showed how great is Your love and brought us hope. I love You, Lord.

HEN Jesus spoke to them saying, "Take courage; it is I, have no fear." — Mt 14:27

Walking on Water

Christ's disciples were terrified to see Him walking on the water. Their boat was several miles off shore. Lord, they thought Your Son was a ghost.

Peter asked to walk on the water, too. "Come!" Christ commanded. And Peter began to walk on the surface of the sea until fear entered his heart. Peter began to sink. Jesus stretched forth His hand and took hold of him, saying, "O you of little faith, why did you doubt?" (Mt 14:31). Lord, our faith is in You and Your Son. I love You, Lord.

HAT shall I render to the Lord for all He has given me? I will take the chalice of salvation and call upon the name of the Lord.

OCT.
31

— Ps 116:12-13

Gifts for God

What can I give to You, Lord, in response for all You have given to me? Everything in existence belongs to You, its Creator. Lord, the answer is simple and clear. I can begin to love You with my whole heart and soul.

You are delighted when I embrace Your holy will. It pleases You when I love all those around me. I show my love when I think kindly of everyone, stop judging, stop condemning, and forgive. Christ explains how we can be pleasing in Your sight. I love You, Lord.

 ND He said to them, "The Son of Man is Lord even of the Sabbath."

NOV.
1

— Lk 6:5

Controversy and Challenge

Is it lawful to heal on the Sabbath? Lord, it would seem totally appropriate to extend Your love on a day dedicated to You. They gathered in a synagogue for prayer. There was a man with a withered hand. Jesus was also present.

Christ asked what they would do if one of their sheep fell into a pit on the Sabbath. "How much more valuable is a person than a sheep. Therefore, it is lawful to do good on the Sabbath" (Mt 12:12). Then Jesus healed the man. Love must always conquer controversy and challenge. I love You, Lord.

159

AGRIPPA said to Paul, "In a little while you would persuade me to become a Christian." — Act 26:28

What Does It Take To Persuade?

Lord, permanent commitments last for a lifetime. With a miraculous catch of fish, Jesus persuaded fishermen to follow Him. They left everything and followed Him.

They walked with Christ, listened to His teachings, and witnessed His miracles. They learned the lesson of love. The Apostles were motivated and gave their lives in service. Lord, You have communicated from the beginning of time. Sending Your Son is the greatest communication. I love You, Lord.

YOU shall say to them: "Thus says the Lord God" . . . and they shall know a Prophet has been in their midst.

— Ezek 2:4-5

Loaves and Fish

It is impossible for anyone to feed five thousand people with five loaves of bread and two fish, unless You, Lord, are with him. Christ had compassion on the multitude. Your Son performed a great miracle and demonstrated His Divinity.

The people's hunger was satisfied, and they were impressed. "This is indeed the Prophet," they exclaimed, "the One Who is to come into the world" (Jn 6:14). The miracles and fulfillment of ancient prophecies won the hearts of many. Their God was near. I love You, Lord.

OR God did not make death, nor does He take pleasure in the destruction of the living. — Wis 1:13

A Funeral

Jesus encountered a large crowd accompanying a widow and the coffin of her only son. Lord, her tears moved Your Son's heart.

He touched the bier. "Young man, I say to you, arise!" (Lk 7:14). To the amazement of all, her son sat up and began to speak. "And Jesus gave him to his mother." Could Jesus have possibly foreseen the great pain His own mother, Mary, would experience when He carried His Cross to Calvary and offered His excruciating death for the world? I love You, Lord.

 E was commanding the unclean spirit to go out of the man. For many times it had hold of him. — Lk 8:29

Demons

Lord, there was a man living among the tombs, possessed by demons. Jesus commanded the evil spirits to leave the man and to enter a herd of swine. The herd ran into the sea and drowned. The swineherds reported the incident throughout the countryside.

The people were terrified and asked Jesus to leave their territory. As Jesus was leaving, the man wished to go with him. But Jesus told him, "Go home and proclaim all that God has done for you" (Lk 8:39). Wherever Jesus went, His love was made known. I love You, Lord.

ESUS came near and touched them, and said, "Arise, and do not be afraid."

— Mt 17:7

NOV.
6

Divine Reassurance

It is surprising, Lord, how often You reassure those You choose to serve You. When their feeling of inadequacy rises to the surface, You tell those that You commission not to fear.

The Angel Gabriel declared, "Do not be afraid, Mary, for you have found grace with God" (Lk 1:30). In a dream, Joseph was told not to fear taking Mary as his wife. When Jesus had risen, He said to His disciples, "Do not fear" (Mt 28:10). Alone we are nothing. With You, all things are possible. I love You, Lord.

 OU shall know that I am the Lord when I open your graves . . . and put My Spirit in you and you shall live.

— Ezek 37:13-14

NOV.
7

From the Dead

The power over life and death belongs exclusively to You, Lord. Jesus called people back to life when they had truly died.

A synagogue official, named Jairus, asked Jesus to come to his twelve-year-old daughter who had passed away. He arrived at the house and took the child by the hand. "Little girl, I say to you, arise!" (Mk 5:41). And she did, walking around the room. The startling news spread throughout the land. In Christ, we see your loving compassion. I love You, Lord.

E set out for Macedonia, being sure that God had called us to preach the Gospel there.

— Act 16:10

Reading the Gospel

When seeds fall on good soil and receive all the proper nutrients, they grow and bear fruit. Jesus told a story about seeds (Mt 13:1-23).

Lord, the seeds are Your words. Many people read the Scriptures. They cover one or more Gospels. Some are convinced of Christ and become Christians. Others close the book with no particular reaction. Nowhere will we find a greater love story. It is Your story, the sending of Your Son for our eternal salvation. I love You, Lord.

OVE one another with mutual affection, anticipating one another with honor.

— Rom 12:10

How To Become a Loving Person

There are steps to take in pursuit of every goal. Becoming a loving person does not happen instantaneously. Lord, You have determined our ultimate challenge, loving You with our whole heart and soul.

We work our way toward heaven by loving our neighbor because in loving him we love You. St. Peter said, "Be all of one mind, compassionate, loving toward one another, merciful, and humble" (1 Pet 3:8). Strengthen our resolve. I love You, Lord.

LL who take refuge in You will be
happy and forever shout for joy.
— Ps 5:12

NOV.
10

Making People Happy

When we love someone we try to make
them happy. Lord, Your Son, Jesus loved His
friends, Martha, Mary, and their brother,
Lazarus.

But one day, when Christ was miles from
Bethany, Lazarus took ill and died. Martha
told Jesus if He was present their brother
would never have passed away. Jesus went to
the cave where he was buried, and in a loud
voice commanded, "Lazarus, come out!" And
the dead man walked. Jesus made His friends
happy. I love You, Lord.

OME trust in chariots, others in horses,
but we trust in the name of the Lord,
our God. — Ps 20:8

NOV.
11

Depending and Trusting

Christ once told a story about a rich fool.
The man had great wealth, abundant har-
vests, and so decided to build bigger barns.
Lord, Your Son, pointed out that material
riches do not go beyond the grave. That very
night the man would die.

"Do not be anxious about your life and
what you will eat or about your body and
what you will wear" (Lk 12:22). The focus
must be on You, Lord. When we truly love
You, our priorities are clear. In our dependency, we trust. I love You, Lord.

OU shall call upon Me, and you shall go; and you shall pray to Me, and I will hear you. — Jer 29:12

Prayerful Inspiration

How to pray and what to pray for! Questions for every age and stage! Lord, we do not always know what is good for us, and You care for us as Your children. St. Paul says, "The Spirit, too, helps our weakness, for we do not know how to pray as we ought" (Rom 8:26).

Lord, with Your inspiration we see love. It is the guidance of the heart and leads to perfect union. How mysterious for us to act freely and to choose to follow You, and yet receive Your motivation and clarification! I love You, Lord.

 ND He, Son though He was, learned obedience from what He suffered. — Heb 5:8

Love and Obedience

Jesus' life was one of love and obedience. From His birth in the stable in Bethlehem to His death on Calvary, Christ loved You, Lord, beyond our comprehension. "He humbled Himself and became obedient unto death; yes, to death on a Cross" (Phil 2:8); "I always do what is pleasing to Him" (Jn 8:29).

Lord, those who profess faith in Christ, His followers, actively seek Your holy will. Christ, the Light of the World, illuminates our path to love You with our whole heart and soul, no further clarification is needed. I love You, Lord.

E showed Himself alive after His suffering by many proofs during forty days. — Act 1:3

Meditation on Christ's Sufferings

Many Saints have been inspired by meditating on Christ's sufferings. They envision His torture, His agony, His rejection. Lord, while these acts are repulsive in themselves, they illustrate the extent of Your Son's love.

Christ was betrayed by one that He loved. He heard false witnesses testifying against Him. While hanging on the Cross, Jesus prayed, "Father, forgive them for they do not know what they are doing" (Lk 23:34). The crucifix is the world's greatest symbol of love. I love You, Lord.

AY the God of patience and of comfort grant you to be of one mind toward each other.— Rom 15:5

God's Patience

No one has more patience than You, Lord. You wait years for hardened hearts to reform. Serious sinners defy Your commandments. They live dangerously, liable for everlasting punishment.

Jesus says, "If you love Me, keep My commandments" (Jn 14:15). Wrongdoers scoff and reject Your love. But, in Your Divine Providence, You know that obstinacy can melt away. Eventually some will say, "O my God, I am heartily sorry for having offended You." How kind, merciful, and loving! I love You, Lord.

ISDOM is glorious and never fades away, and is easily seen by those who love her, and found by those who seek her. — Wis 6:13

The Gift of Wisdom

One of the gifts of the Holy Spirit is wisdom. This blessing enables a person to discern clearly what is truly valuable. Lord, we are wise to seek Your will. This wonderful grace clarifies our goals and guides our choices. Wisdom aligns our lives with Your wishes.

If we comprehend our origin and our destiny, that is wisdom. If we are convinced in our hearts that happiness lies with You alone, that is wisdom. Is there any other enlightenment more meritorious and deserving? I love You, Lord.

———————

HE Lord is my strength; . . . therefore, with my will I give Him praise. — Ps 28:7

Mysterious But Beautiful

Lord, it will always be mysterious how You endowed us with free will and yet Your holy will is always accomplished. We may not understand fully, but we do well to recognize reality.

Stage and screen can render great service by illustrating. We are both entertained and enlightened. Nevertheless the root and origin of every poem, song, and novel derives from You. You fashioned human beings after your image and likeness. Truth calls us to praise and acknowledge You. I love You, Lord.

ET all Your works give You thanks, O
Lord, and let Your faithful ones bless
You. — Ps 145:10

Love and Thanks

Giving thanks is a recognition of goodness,
an acknowledgement. Favors are easily recognized. Lord, parents teach their children to
say "thanks."

St. Paul says, "In all things give thanks, for
this is the will of God for you in Christ Jesus"
(1 Thes 5:18). Jesus gave You thanks when He
multiplied the loaves and fish to feed thousands. Everyone is blessed when they appreciate You as the God of love. I love You, Lord.

AY He grant you to know Christ's
love, which surpasses knowledge
that you may be filled unto the
fullness of God. — Eph 3:16, 19

Most Loving Person

At a point of time in history You, heavenly
Father, sent Your Son. "The Word became
flesh and dwelt among us" (Jn 1:14). People
came to know what love is all about.

Christ's entire life demonstrated this. Wit-
nesses saw Jesus carry His Cross, fall beneath
its weight, and struggle to the top of Calvary.
Love went beyond limits, to the last drop of
His Precious Blood. No one has loved us more.
This conviction conquers all challenges. I love
You, Lord.

ND when the Angel came to her, he said, "Hail, full of grace, the Lord is with you. Blessed are you among women." — Lk 1:28

Full of Grace

The term "full of grace" is immediately identified with Mary, the Mother of Jesus. Lord, in her identification with her Son's life, passion, and death, she was one with You.

"By her obedience, her faith, her hope, and her burning love, she cooperated in a way that was quite unique, in the work of the Savior. . . . She is therefore a mother to us in the order of grace" (Vatican II: *Constitution on the Church*, 61). I love You, Lord.

ESUS Christ . . . is at the right hand of God, swallowing up death that we might be made heirs of eternal life. — 1 Pet 3:21-22

Conquering Death

Love conquers death. If Adam and Eve had not sinned, there would be no dying. Lord, it is clear that death is a consequence of original sin. But Christ promised eternal life. He came to our world to redeem us.

Jesus declared, "I am the Resurrection" (Jn 11:25). Our faith in a loving God overcomes fear. "Whoever believes in the Son has everlasting life" (Jn 3:36). Jesus surrendered His life that we might live and love forever. Happiness is to be with You. I love You, Lord.

ITH everlasting kindness have I had mercy on you, says the Lord.
— Isa 54:8

How Long Does God's Kindness Endure?

Lord, will You ever tire of loving us? Will Your patience run thin and become exhausted? When we begin to comprehend that You are love itself, then our understanding has inched forward.

The Bible tells of Your wrath, Your anger over sin. It also relates Your forgiveness. We have reason to rejoice. "Give thanks to the Lord, Who is good, for His kindness endures forever" (1 Chr 16:34). We can depend on Your love. I love You, Lord.

HEY must be present each morning to thank and praise the Lord, and also in the evening. — 1 Chr 23:30

How Often?

Those in love are strengthened by assurances. They say, "I love you" and their bonds become more secure. Lord, it is completely logical that we should affirm our love for You often—e.g., by morning and evening prayers.

The day becomes sanctified by prayer, conversation with You. This good habit reflects our recognition of Your loving presence. Men and women who lift their minds and hearts prayerfully are in touch. We are mindful of our special calling. I love You, Lord.

ECAUSE you have been faithful in a little matter, you shall have charge over ten towns. — Lk 19:17

Little Ways

Lord, You appreciate all the little ways we find to express our appreciation and love. Parents bathe and clothe and play with their children. Cooking, cleaning, and help with homework, send positive messages to them.

Families pray together morning and evening, and worship hand in hand on Sundays. The relationship develops cultivated by countless kindnesses. These generous gestures speak to You, Lord, because whatever is done for another is done for You, too. I love You, Lord.

BLESSED is everyone who fears the Lord, who walks in His ways. — Ps 128:1

More Little Ways

Lord, Christmas cards and thank-you notes fly through the mail like Angels carrying tokens of affection. Phone calls and E-mail bridge separations. We serve You when we send our love to others. This means that we are thinking about others.

The short prayers men and women offer as they go through their days tell You something, too. Praise, petition, honor and glory wing their way heavenward. We are thinking of You, our loving Lord. I love You, Lord.

ET the little children come to Me, . . .
for of such is the kingdom of God.

— Mk 10:14

Hugs

Lord, a hug from a child is worth more than a million dollars, especially if she is one's child. Little boys and girls quite simply win more hearts than public relations courses.

What delight Jesus must have experienced when the children gathered around Him! The kingdom of heaven is open to the likes of little children, He explained. Inspire us to become like these little ones that we may receive Your love and one day enter Your kingdom. I love You, Lord.

HINKING these things within myself, I pondered in my heart that to be allied to wisdom is immortality.

— Wis 8:17

Contemplation

Lord, when do You speak to the heart? It would seem that You can hardly get a word in edgewise. There are some people who have the radio and television playing from morning to night. Thoughts of You are crowded out.

To have a relationship with You, people must designate occasions for silence. There is a hunger and a thirst for happiness within every person. Our souls find rest and peace in union with You. Contemplatives ponder Your greatness and Your love. I love You, Lord.

FOR [wisdom] is an infinite treasure to men, and those that use it become friends of God. — Wis 7:14

Winning Friends

There are books and courses on how to influence people and gain friends. Lord, the best program ever devised is clearly outlined by Your Son, Jesus. If His commands are embodied, success is guaranteed.

Very simply it is to love everyone, the difficult, the haughty, the contentious, the contrary. In fact, it is to love our enemies—something easier said than done. Becoming a Christian in the true sense of the word is a great challenge. I love You, Lord.

A GLAD heart makes a cheerful face, but by grief of mind the spirit is cast down. — Prov 15:13

The Effort To Be Cheerful

Love comes in different shapes and sizes. Lord, in our daily contacts, smiles and pleasantries count. They say something good to those we meet. At the gas station, at the checkout, over the phone, our words set the tone.

When someone is rude, a soft answer turns away wrath. A sympathetic reply calms a troubled soul. In a manner of speaking, love is communicated. "God loves a cheerful giver" (2 Cor 9:7). Everybody else loves a cheerful character, too. I love You, Lord.

WILL praise the Lord with all my heart in the company of the just, in the congregation.
— Ps 111:1

Praising the Lord

Some people regard prayer as a very private engagement, and it is. But surely not limited to the privacy of our rooms. Lord, You deserve to be acknowledged everywhere and at all times.

The Psalmist declares, "Praise the Lord; the Lord is good! Sing to God's name; it is sweet!" (Ps 135:3). This presupposes enthusiasm, verve, and exuberance. When a person begins to appreciate Your unspeakable love, he breaks out in praise. I love You, Lord.

ND I heard the voice of many Angels round about the throne, and the living creatures and the elders.
— Rev 5:11

Joining the Choirs of Angels

Lord, the heavenly choir sang in Bethlehem at Christ's birth. "Peace on earth! Good will to men!" At Mass, during the preface, worshipers say they join the Angels in praising. St. Augustine suggests we double our praise with song.

How important to render fitting honor. Inspire parishioners in every parish to join the angelic choir. The Eucharistic liturgy is at the center of our relationship. Churchgoers unite with Your Son, as He offers Himself in sacrifice. I love You, Lord.

WILL be the God of all the families of Israel, and they shall be My people.

— Jer 31:1

DEC. 2

Family Prayer

Lord, children learn to love You at home. The relationship that their parents have with You is shared. How pleasing it must be for You to see good mothers and fathers kneeling with their children in prayer!

Mothers and fathers communicate values. How important it is to worship! They explain our origin, that You are the Giver of life itself. Destiny, too! The children come to know the very purpose of life is to love You. I love You, Lord.

 E who loves God should love his brothers also.

— 1 Jn 4:21

DEC. 3

Happiest Person

Who is the world's happiest person? Somebody in love, to be sure. Lord, there is no doubt. You love every man, woman, and child. You have enough love to go around and love each one of us individually.

Once we recognize this reality, our attitude brightens. We begin to love You in return. "If anyone loves Me, he will keep My word," Jesus said, "and My Father will love him, and We will come to him and make Our abode with him" (Jn 14:23). I love You, Lord.

HO shall know Your thought, unless You give wisdom, and send Your Holy Spirit from above?

— Wis 9:17

Telling God What To Do

Lord, it is never a good idea to tell You what to do. It is the height of haughtiness. Your Son explained that You exalt the humble and humble the exalted.

When things do not go our way, we need to consider Your Divine Providence. When You overrule our wishes, it is done in a loving way. Free choice should always bow to an omniscient, loving God. There is serenity when we actually welcome Your holy will. There is wisdom in resignation. I love You, Lord.

 AKE known to me, O Lord, my end, and the measure of my days, that I may know how frail I am.

— Ps 39:5

Eternity in Mind

Lord, even if we limit our thinking to this world, You always have eternity in mind. From morning until night, our thoughts are on the thousands of details that go with daily living. You are mindful of every person on earth.

How blessed are those who pray and orient themselves as people of faith! Consciously, those who believe are working out their salvation. They are going somewhere, not just wandering through life. Their destiny is an all-loving God. I love You, Lord.

IRECT me in Your truth and teach me, for You are God my Savior.

— Ps 25:5

Elusive Truth

Lord, the human mind is darkened. When Adam and Eve sinned they brought about conditions that have not gone away.

Discovering truth does not only depend on intellectual keenness, but also on dispositions of soul. Seeds do not germinate, and plants do not grow, unless the soil is conducive. Lives are lived in denial if we refuse to conform and to reform. "I am the Way, and the Truth, and the Life," Christ declared (Jn 14:6). We need Your grace. I love You, Lord.

 N that day He shall come to be glorified in His Saints, and to be marveled at in all who have believed.

— 2 Thes 1:10

All Saints' Day

Critics of Halloween run the risk of scorn. Lord, there is a reversal of mind and heart commemorating the eve of All Hallows, or All Saints' Day. The focus is on the bizarre, the ghoulish, the weird. The Saints are all but forgotten.

Nevertheless the feast commemorates those who have come to love You perfectly. The commemoration goes all the way back to the year 610 A.D. calling to mind all those in heaven with You. I love You, Lord.

EAR, for I will speak of great things, and my lips shall be opened to preach right things. — Prov 8:6

Teaching Morality

Right or wrong does not depend on an individual's choice. Lord, You determine morality. Your will is without dispute.

Nevertheless, the relativists say, "What is right for you may not be right for me. No one knows all the answers. Who are you to tell me what to do?" You are the Supreme Being. So we welcome Your commandments. They are blessings. They lead us to You. Clarify our thoughts so we may love You wholeheartedly. I love You, Lord.

LL that is born of God overcomes the world; and this is the victory that overcomes the world, our faith. — 1 Jn 5:4

How To Succeed

On the night before He died, Jesus said to His Apostles, "As the Father has loved Me, so I also have loved you. Abide in My love. If you keep My commandments, you will abide in My love" (Jn 15:9-10).

Lord, He wished to impress His followers. The bond that would keep them together, that would help them succeed, was love. This means embracing Your commandments as if there was no other way in the world to live. I love You, Lord.

OW I . . . am convinced with regard to you that you yourselves are full of love. — Rom 15:14

DEC. 10

Mother Theresa

Reportedly the last words of one of the world's most dedicated caregivers, Mother Theresa of Calcutta, were "I love You, Jesus."

There was no doubt in her mind about her vocation. She took Jesus' admonition literally: "As long as you did it for one of these least brothers of Mine, you did it for Me" (Mt 25:40). When asked how she could work in such demanding conditions, in squalor and poverty for the most destitute, she smiled and said, "Love them." I love You, Lord.

 ND I will repay them according to their deeds. — Jer 25:14

DEC. 11

Dedication and Deeds

Love is not a flight of fancy. It is not contained in slushy romances published in magazines. Lord, love shows its true colors in dedication and deeds.

Parents tell love stories when they pray with their children, walk to church with them, and kneel in worship. Consistent caring paints a more accurate picture. Feeding the hungry, giving drink to the thirsty, sheltering the homeless—all the corporal works of mercy embrace Your holy will. I love You, Lord.

HE Lord has sworn and He will not repent: "You are a priest forever."

— Ps 110:4

Ordained

"You are a priest forever." Once ordained, there is an indelible mark on a soul. A priest is a man chosen to offer sacrifice officially. Lord, there is only one, true priest. It is Your Son, Jesus Christ.

He is both priest and victim at the Eucharistic Sacrifice. By Divine design the human priest speaks in the first person of Jesus Christ. "This is My Body. . . . This is the cup of My Blood. . . ." It is mysterious how the one ordained acts intimately in Jesus' name. I love You, Lord.

AM the light of the world. He who follows Me does not walk in darkness.

— Jn 8:12

The Light of the World

God has revealed truths that could never be known merely through reason. The Old Testament and New Testament Books in the Bible record Your communication. Your voice carries through the centuries.

The greatest revelation came with Your Son, Jesus. He established His Church to help interpret Your word. Your grace clarifies our thoughts. Life is a journey, but Jesus, the Light of the World, dispels the darkness. I love You, Lord.

ND indeed in this present state we groan, desiring to be clothed with our heavenly dwelling. — 2 Cor 5:2

Wanting To Love

The greatest commandment is to love You, Lord, with our whole heart and soul. The success of one's lifetime depends on its fulfillment. Lord, it is only through personal desire and dedication that this is going to come true. We must want to love You.

The goal must be clarified both in mind and in heart. It will not be attained through an occasional or a casual relationship. Everything is fleeting in this passing world. But the one stable factor that overrides disappointments and failures is loving You. This is our sustaining strength. I love You, Lord.

E shall read it all the days of his life, that he may learn to fear the Lord. — Deut 17:19

Learning To Love

"It is not good for man to be alone" (Gen 2:18). So, Lord, You created a suitable partner for Adam, and called her Eve. Adam needed a helpmate, someone with whom to share. Love does not exist in a vacuum.

The ideal is to relate to each other lovingly. People who love place others ahead of themselves. This does not happen automatically. This is a practiced art much like mastering a musical instrument. It takes time to make beautiful music. I love You, Lord.

WE no person anything except to love one another; for whoever loves his neighbor has fulfilled the Law.
— Rom 13:8

A Commandment

Lord, Your Son, said, "This is My commandment, that you love one another as I have loved you" (Jn 15:12). This was on the night before Jesus died. That people should love one another was not new. It was contained in Scripture through the centuries.

How much do I love you? I am about to shed the last drop of My Precious Blood! How should you love other men and women? Totally! Without question and without hesitation! I love You, Lord.

AM the Good Shepherd, and I know Mine and they know Me.
— Jn 10:14

Christ's Signature

"I am the Good Shepherd. The Good Shepherd lays down His life for His sheep" (Jn 10:11). Christ's sacrifice was total. He shed the last drop of His Precious Blood. This impassioned statement is, so to speak, Jesus' signature.

Many of His true followers would all too willingly sign their names in the blood of martyrdom. They would offer Him love for love and sacrifice for sacrifice. The first three centuries are called "The Age of Martyrs." I love You, Lord.

I N His love and in His mercy He redeemed them, and He carried them and lifted them up. — Isa 63:9

How Great Is God's Love?

It is impossible to measure Your love, Lord, because, like Yourself, Your love is infinite. This is quite beyond our thinking. How can our limited minds comprehend Your limitless capacity?

There are no preconditions to Your love. No such thing as a prenuptial agreement. No fine print! Strange though, that we always expect this kind of love from You. Our love falters. We hesitate and set limits. How great is Your love! I love You, Lord.

 E said, "Behold your mother." And from that hour the disciple took her into his home. — Jn 19:27

Passion Play

Lord, there is a story about a passion play. On stage, Judas, tortured by guilt, throws the thirty pieces of silver to the floor. He cries out, "What shall I do? Where shall I go?"

A child in the audience responds aloud, "Why doesn't he go to the Blessed Mother?" There is no fear through Mary's mediation. Perhaps the child's recommendation is a stroke of genius. Christ's followers have a special relationship with Mary, the Mother of Jesus. While on the Cross, Christ entrusted all of us to her. I love You, Lord.

O them God willed to make known how rich in glory is this mystery among the Gentiles.

DEC.
20

— Col 1:27

Good Policy!

There is only one plan for salvation. There is only one policy that can make the world turn smoothly. Lord, no one can improve on Your commandments. They are an expression of Your holy will. Who knows better what works and what does not work?

Peace and harmony flow when human relationships are founded on true love. Who commits crime? Who declares war? Who is guilty of violence? Surely not someone who listens to You. I love You, Lord.

HOEVER humbles himself as this little child, he is the greatest in the kingdom of heaven.

DEC.
21

— Mt 18:4

Humility and Truth

Each person seeks individuality. This expresses itself as we grow up. Lord, every little step in the maturing process is like a declaration of independence. We long to do "our thing."

How good it is for us to recognize our limitations! Conformity to Your holy will is more blessed than any attempt at rugged individuality. Pride clouds our vision. Honesty brings real perspective. Touch our souls with Your grace. I love You, Lord.

O shall you do them in the land you shall possess. And you shall observe, and fulfill them in practice.

DEC. 22

— Deut 4:5-6

Practice! Practice! Practice!

Good habits are called virtues. Bad habits, vices. Lord, concentration and perseverance bring favorable results. Natural abilities can be honed and cultivated in time. Music lessons make virtuosos through practice!

There is no greater virtue than love. Every day there are opportunities to be kind. Deliberate acts of generosity help to mold character. Love becomes part of our being. Christians should be focused on You. I love You, Lord.

 UT in praying, do not multiply words as the Gentiles do. . . . For your Father knows what you need before you ask Him.

DEC. 23

— Mt 6:7-8

Brief Exchanges

Attention spans are limited. We have restricted powers of concentration. Lord, living in this highly sophisticated world, we have become accustomed to the sound bite. Radio and television bombard us with messages.

Long conversations with You may prove challenging, too. Most of us do better praying more often. "I love You" is a short prayer. Sometimes these brief exchanges are quite spontaneous, particularly when we are in trouble. "Be with me, Lord." I love You, Lord.

IVE to the Lord the glory of His name; adore the Lord in holy attire.

— Ps 29:2

Whose Glory?

Lord, there is always a temptation to think we have great ideas. And an even greater temptation to believe we can survive quite well by ourselves. When things go well, people are not as inclined to kneel in prayer.

Hardship and scarcity move people to storm heaven, to pray more. Paradoxically, we are better off suffering want when eternity is in the balance. How realistic to attribute all our blessings to You! Glory be Yours! I love You, Lord.

 E is mindful of His covenant forever, the promise that He made to a thousand generations.

— Ps 105:8

A Forever Relationship

Permanent commitments are hard to come by these days. People are hesitant to commit themselves. Lord, this is not the case with You. Your Son, Jesus, too, totally commits Himself.

"I am the living Bread that has come down from heaven; whoever eats this bread shall live forever" (Jn 6:51). Christ fulfilled the promise at the Last Supper. The Holy Eucharist! Through this Sacrament Your Son cultivates and nourishes His loving relationship. I love You, Lord.

THEY shall know that I, the Lord, their God, am with them, and that they are My people. — Ezek 34:30

Genuine Relationship

Lord, the Psalmist tells us that a fool declares there is no God. History records Your communication with people from the beginning of time. Jesus demonstrated by His teachings and miracles both His Divinity and His Humanity. Emmanuel! God is with us!

Pity the person who has not developed a personal relationship through prayer, conversation with You. No man is an island! We are social beings and need one another. We are Your children and we need You. I love You, Lord.

LESS the Lord always and ask Him . . . to make all your endeavors successful. — Tob 4:19

If God Is for Us

Never bet on a sure thing. This is clearly an unfair advantage. Lord, it is like stealing when we wager without the possibility of losing. We know something our opponent does not.

The same cannot be said when we trust in You. St. Paul says, "If God is for us, who is against us?" (Rom 8:31). And there is actually no gamble, no chance of failure. There is absolute certitude that You love us. This inspires confidence. God listens. You can bet on it. I love You, Lord.

THUS, the priest shall make atonement for the sin that was committed.

— Lev 5:13

DEC. 28

Love Atones

Charity covers a multitude of sins. The underlying basis for sin is the lack of love. Lord, a person can turn his life around with the help of Your grace. There are no hopeless cases.

Once a Pharisee invited Jesus to his home. A sinful woman entered. She bathed Christ's feet with her tears and dried them with her hair. How pleased He must have been with her change of heart! It is good to know that the reversal of a lifetime can atone for wrongdoing. I love You, Lord.

ND other sheep I have. . . . Them also I must bring . . . and there shall be one flock and one shepherd.

— Jn 10:16

DEC. 29

A Gift

What can we give to the Lord? Lord, it is difficult purchasing presents for men and women who have everything. And You, Lord, own whatever exists. What will please You?

Among the many wishes on Your list, Christian unity has to be close to the top. In His Last Supper discourse, Jesus prayed for unity of faith. As history evolved, religious denominations have multiplied scandalously. May we love all who bear the name of Christian. I love You, Lord.

G O, therefore, and make disciples of all nations.

— Mt 28:19

DEC. 30

Another Gift

There are hundreds of religions in this world. Lord, You wish all people, whether believers or not, to love one another.

Most people on this planet do not know Your Son, Jesus. His coming is the world's greatest love story. "God loved the world so much that He gave His only Son" (Jn 3:16). Evangelization is the essential mission of the Church. Whatever we can do to communicate this Faith is indeed a gift of love. I love You, Lord.

L OVE the Lord your God, and walk in all His ways . . . and cleave to Him.

— Jos 22:5

DEC. 31

Nothing Else But Love

Lord, if a person believes that there is nothing else more noble than loving You, he has arrived at an excellent conclusion. He entertains absolute truth.

When we receive the Body and Blood of Christ in Holy Communion there is a perfect and intimate communication between heaven and earth. Quicken us that our love for You may grow stronger. "Let everything that breathes praise the Lord. Alleluia!" (Ps 150:6). I love You, Lord.

Prayer to Achieve
Inner Peace

SLOW me down, Lord.
Ease the pounding of my heart
by the quieting of my mind.
Steady my hurried pace
with a vision of the eternal reach of time.
Give me, amid the confusion of the day,
the calmness of the everlasting hills.
Break the tensions of my nerves and muscles
with the soothing music of the singing streams
that live in memory.

Help me to know the magical,
restoring power of sleep.
Teach me the art of taking minute vacations
—of slowing down to look at a flower,
to chat with a friend,
to pat a dog,
to read a few lines from a good book.

Slow me down, Lord.

Prayer for the Family

LORD God,
from You every family in heaven
and on earth takes its name.
Father, you are Love and Life.

Through Your Son, Jesus Christ,
born of woman, and through the Holy Spirit,
fountain of divine charity,
grant that every family on earth
may become for each successive generation
a true shrine of life and love.

Grant that Your grace may guide the thoughts and
    actions
of husbands and wives
for the good of their families
and of all the families in the world.

Grant that the young may find in the family
solid support for their human dignity
and for their growth in truth and love.

Grant that love,
strengthened by the Sacrament of marriage,
may prove mightier than all the weaknesses and trials
through which our families sometimes pass.

Through the intercession of the Holy Family of
    Nazareth,
grant that the Church may fruitfully carry out
her worldwide mission in and through the family.
Through Christ our Lord, Who is the Way, the Truth
    and the Life
for ever and ever. Amen. *Pope John Paul II*

Prayer in Praise of the Triune God

I venerate and glorify You,
O most Blessed Trinity,
in union with that ineffable glory
with which God the Father,
in His omnipotence,
honors the Holy Spirit forever.

I magnify and bless You,
O most Blessed Trinity,
in union with that most reverent glory
with which God the Son,
in His unsearchable wisdom,
glorifies the Father and the Holy Spirit forever.

I adore and extol You,
O most Blessed Trinity,
in union with that most adequate and befitting glory
with which the Holy Spirit,
in His unchangeable goodness,
extols the Father and the Son forever.

The Glory Be

Glory to the Father,
and to the Son,
and to the Holy Spirit.
As it was in the beginning,
is now, and will be forever.

OTHER OUTSTANDING BOOKS IN THIS SERIES

LEAD, KINDLY LIGHT—By Rev. James Sharp. Minute meditations for every day of the year taken from the writings of Cardinal Newman plus a concluding prayer for each day.　　**No. 184**

EVERY DAY IS A GIFT—Introduction by Most Rev. Frederick Schroeder. Popular meditations for every day, featuring a text from Sacred Scripture, a quotation from the writings of a Saint, and a meaningful prayer.　　**No. 195**

LARGE TYPE EDITION—This popular book offered in large, easy-to-read print.　　**No. 196**

MARY DAY BY DAY—Minute meditations for every day of the year, including a Scripture passage, a quotation from the Saints, and a concluding prayer. Printed in two colors with over 300 illustrations.　　**No. 180**

MINUTE MEDITATIONS FROM THE POPES—By Rev. Jude Winkler, OFM Conv. Minute meditations for every day of the year using the words of twentieth-century Popes. Printed and illustrated in two colors.　　**No. 175**

AUGUSTINE DAY BY DAY—By Rev. John Rotelle, O.S.A. Minute meditations for every day of the year taken from the writings of Augustine, with a concluding prayer also from the Saint.　　**No. 170**

BIBLE DAY BY DAY—By Rev. John Kersten, S.V.D. Minute Bible meditations for every day including a short Scripture text and brief reflection. Printed in two colors with 300 illustrations.　　**No. 150**

LIVING WISDOM FOR EVERY DAY—By Rev. Bennet Kelley, C.P. Choice texts from St. Paul of the Cross, one of the true Masters of Spirituality, and a prayer for each day.　　**No. 182**

MINUTE MEDITATIONS FOR EACH DAY—By Rev. Bede Naegele, O.C.D. This very attractive book offers a short Scripture text, a practical reflection, and a meaningful prayer for each day of the year.　　**No. 190**

www.catholicbookpublishing.com

ISBN 978-1-937913-05-2

9 781937 913052

90000